Primary Art

It's the Process, Not the Product

More titles by MaryAnn F. Kohl, published by Gryphon House, Inc.

First Art: Art Experiences for Toddlers and Twos

Preschool Art

Preschool Art mini-series (5 individual titles: Drawing, Painting, Collage, Craft, Clay)

Making Make-Believe

The Big Messy Art Book

MathArts, with Cindy Gainer

Cooking Art, with Jean Potter

Global Art, with Jean Potter

More titles by MaryAnn F. Kohl, published by Bright Ring Publishing, Inc.

Storybook Art, with Jean Potter

Discovering Great Artists, with Kim Solga

Science Arts, with Jean Potter

Good Earth Art, with Cindy Gainer

Mudworks

Mudworks Bilingual Edition

Scribble Art

Readers can find out more about MaryAnn Kohl, her books, and her interests at her website www.brightring.com. She enjoys hearing from readers, and especially from young artists.

A MARYANN F. KOHL BOOK

Primary ART

It's the Process, Not the Product

MaryAnn F. Kohl

Illustrations by Rebecca Van Slyke

gryphon house®, inc.
Beltsville, MD

Bulk Purchase

Gryphon House books are available for special premiums and sales promotions as well as for fundraising use. Special editions or book excerpts can be created to specification. For details, contact the Director of Marketing at the Gryphon House address.

Copyright

© 2005 MaryAnn F. Kohl

Published by Gryphon House, Inc.
PO Box 207, Beltsville MD 20704
800-638-0928
www.gryphonhouse.com or www.brightring.com
Printed in the United States of America

Library of Congress Cataloging in Publication Data

Kohl, MaryAnn F.
  Primary art : it's the process, not the product / by MaryAnn Kohl ;
illustrations by Rebecca Van Slyke.
      p. cm.
  Includes index.
  Summary: "Over 100 art projects that teachers of children ages five to eight can do in the classroom. Also applicable to parents and other caregivers"--Provided by publisher.
  ISBN: 978-87659-283-0
  1. Art--Study and teaching (Primary)--Activity programs. I. Title.
  N361.K64 2005
  372.5'044--dc22
                                         2005001916

Gryphon House is a member of the Green Press Initiative, a nonprofit program dedicated to supporting publishers in their efforts to reduce their use of fiber-sourced forests. This book is made of 30% post-consumer waste. For further information visit www.greenpressinitiative.org.

Dedication

In memory of my bright and loving mother, Betty Louise Fritzlen Faubion Clement (1924-1981), who gave me gifts to last a lifetime: bedtime stories and books, time to imagine and pretend, art supplies and music lessons, bikes and swings and forts, belief in the golden rule, a standard of responsibility and determination, a warm lap and loving arms.

> *I found I could say things with color and shapes that I couldn't say any other way—things I had no words for.*
>
> —Georgia O'Keeffe, artist
> (1887–1986)

Acknowledgments

Many fine and dedicated educators inspired creative art activities in *Primary Art*, and are acknowledged with appreciation and admiration below. Thank you to each one for contributing to art education through their classrooms and their willingness to share ideas through this book:

Ann Heineman, Columbus, Ohio: Mini-Master, p. 52

Beth Elzinga, Waltham, Vermont: True Resist, p. 63

Carola Dunham, Pacoima, California: Winter Village, p. 165

Cathy Gaul, Cherry Hill, New Jersey: Gloss Watercolor, p. 59

Cindy Caporaso, New Providence, New Jersey: Scribble Dribble, p. 70

Dayna B. Wolf, Potomac, Maryland: Plaster ideas in general

Deb Sterner, Angola, New York: Wavy Grid, p. 39

Denise Pannell, Defiance, Ohio: Puffy Stained Glass, p. 34

Ellen Sears, Anchorage, Kentucky: Crystal Winter, Shimmer Paint, p. 74 & 58

Sky McClain, Moorestown, New Jersey: Paper Weave, p. 123

Ingrid Crowther, Edmonton, Alberta, Canada: Windy Bead Mobile, p. 154

James Ray, Somerville, Texas: Simple Grid Enlargement, p. 25

Jan [Last name unknown], City, Arizona: Sparkly Layered Snow, p. 75

Jana Way, Thorntown, Indiana: Winter Village, p. 165

Jeryl Hollingsworth, Anderson, South Carolina: Foil Figure, p. 141

Linda Eastman, Livonia, Michigan: Foil Squeezy, p. 140

MaryAnn Woelfel, Menomonee Falls, Wisconsin: Foil Shimmer Mosaic, p. 117

Mary-Anne Schoenike, Shawano, Wisconsin: Expressly My Book, p. 103

Michal Austin, Potwin, Kansas: Glue Line Design, Shadow Shapes, p. 77

Patti Caiola, Toledo, Ohio: Optigraph, p. 115

Paulie Schenkelberg, Vancouver, Washington: Warmed Leaves, p. 99

Peggi R. Stevens, Blue Hill, Maine: Tatami Shoji Screen, p. 173

Roberta Dunkel, Jefferson City, Missouri: Chalk ideas in general

Rona Somers, Sunrise, Florida: Shiny Foil Depiction, p. 35

Teri Schlotman, Ft. Mitchell, Kentucky: Shimmer Paint, p. 58

Tina Grimes, Defiance, Ohio: Master of Parody, p. 53

Valerie Kerwin, Sarasota, Florida: Fine Art Scenes, p. 51

Weezie Johnson, Houston, Texas: Mosaics, p. 117

Special Acknowledgments

Fine educators make a difference every day through their contributions and generosity as they go above and beyond the norm making the educational lives of children bright and exciting:

Rebecca Van Slyke—second grade teacher and book illustrator, Lynden/Bellingham, Washington. Rebecca helped to organize many of the initial projects in *Primary Art*. Her sense of creativity and her knowledge of art with children are a great benefit to me. Rebecca generously shares her classroom—and her daughter—for participation in and testing of art experiments and projects, confirming that our art ideas are successful with real kids.

Linda Woods—art teacher, St. John's School, Houston, Texas. Linda has often generously offered her help, her ideas, and her students' works, both for *Primary Art* and for *Storybook Art*. See Linda's students' work at www.sjs.org/arts/lower/gallery.asp?bhcp=1 and www.princetonol.com/groups/iad/lessons/elem/.

Michal Austin—art teacher, Flinthills Primary, Cassoday, Kansas. Michal has kindly offers her expertise in art, as well as her students' work, both for *Primary Art* and for *Storybook Art*. See Michal's students' work at www.geocities.com/theartkids/artlessons.html and www.princetonol.com/groups/iad/lessons/elem/.

Judy Decker—art educator, Lima, Ohio. Judy is the Webmaster of Incredible Art Department and Incredible Art Resources, and has been kind and generous as she freely distributes humor and insight to all. Judy has been astoundingly instrumental in offering help on many levels of art education to many people. In particular, Judy has assisted and facilitated fair representation of contributors to *Primary Art*. Judy maintains the finest art education website on the Internet, The Incredible Art Department www.princetonol.com/groups/iad/ where her art resources can be enjoyed. View her unique Pueblo bird art activity at www.princetonol.com/groups/iad/Files/birds.htm.

Ken Rohrer——founder, Incredible Art Department. (Education Coordinator, Indiana Humanities Council). Ken created the Incredible Art Department www.princetonol.com/groups/iad/, not only the finest art education website on the Internet, but a significant gift to educators of children of all ages. Read about Ken and the history of the website at www.princetonol.com/groups/iad/history/history.html.

Young Artists

Twenty bright young illustrators and artists contributed their creative artworks to *Primary Art*, enhancing the clarity and inspiration of illustrations throughout the book. Not only are these young people excellent artists, they also cheerfully met deadlines and reworked images with dedication to suit the format of the book. Tremendous thanks and appreciation go to:

Abby Brandt, age 7, grade 2, Poulsbo, WA: Foil Shimmer Mosaic, p. 117

Andy Brandt, age 5, grade K, Poulsbo, WA: To the Letter Collage, p. 132

Cameron Hagins, age 7, grade 2, Lynden, WA: Clipped Inset, p. 44

Carley Roddy, age 10, grade 4, Lynden, WA: Spray & Scrape Resist, p. 18

Chelsea Whitener, age 12, grade 7, Everson, WA: Tempera Chalk, p. 42

Dakoda Bradley, age 10, grade 4, Nooksack, WA: Penciled Watercolor, p. 16

Daniel Ashworth, age 9, grade 4, Lynden, WA: Associated Clay, p. 152

David Castañeda, age 8, grade 2, Lynden, WA: Surreal Clipping, p. 45

Emily Riddle, age 7, grade 2, Lynden, WA: Chalk Walk, p. 40

Geoffrey Linn, age 11, grade 6, Leavenworth, WA: Simple Grid Enlargement, p. 25

Jacob VanBerkum, age 8, grade 2, Everson, WA: Geo Art, p. 100

Kayla Comstock, age 10, grade 4, Lynden, WA: RAD, p. 65

Kayla Johnston, age 10, grade 4, Lynden, WA: Oil Pastel Resist, p. 61

Kira Niemi, age 8, grade 2, Everson, WA: Glue Line Relief, p. 89

Lauren Roddy, age 6, grade K, Lynden, WA: Glue Line Design, p. 71

Molly Brandt, age 9, grade 4, Poulsbo, WA: Brain Waves, p. 102

Morgan Van Slyke, age 9, grade 4, Bellingham, WA: Photocopy Repeat; Posed Imitation, pp. 50 & 51

Noah Bartz, age 7, grade 2, Lynden, WA: Half & Half Art, p. 27

Sarah Hunnicutt, age 5, grade K, Anderson, IN: Natural Painting; Knock, Knock, Build It, pp. 78 & 164

Shane Treloar, age 10, grade 4, Lynden, WA: Series Cartooning, p. 21

Taylor VanDalen, age 10, grade 4, Lynden, WA: Master of Parody, p. 53

Weston Whitener, age 9, grade 4, Everson, WA: Great Art & Me, p. 111

Table of Contents

TABLE OF CONTENTS

Introduction

"It's the process, not the product."

Elementary-aged children continue to manipulate their worlds as they have done since toddlerhood when they first poked a finger into a lump of playdough, pushed a crayon across paper, or dabbed paint on newsprint. Now that the children are older, what has changed? Older children state that they are looking for "results" from their creative endeavors while maintaining their individual creative integrity. Our job as parents and educators is to provide art activities that are truly art, not just crafts—art that has integrity in technique, materials, and *satisfying results*. The "process, not product" philosophy was never more true for children ages 5 to 10, but with this addition: "Art: It's the process and *unique results*, not the product."

Just what does it mean when we say children want satisfying results? These artists are ready for and desire impressive creative results, aesthetically pleasing artistic results, and evidence of the fine-tuning of their artistic skills. In the most simple terms, elementary-aged children want their art to "look good" while remaining uniquely their own. They like their art to be one of a kind and an expression of their own creativity, but they want it to look aesthetically pleasing. Some of the words elementary-aged children have used to describe this kind of art are "fancy," "amazing," "awesome," "interesting," and "special." To say they expect results is to reinforce the philosophy of exploring and experimenting with art, but using their refined skills and abilities to control the results.

Children from kindergarten through third grade will continue to benefit creatively as they explore, experiment, and discover the possibilities of how art materials

Every child is an artist. The problem is how to remain an artist once we grow up…It took me four years to paint like Raphael, but a lifetime to paint like a child.

—Pablo Picasso, artist (1881–1973)

behave and transform; to find their unique pathways through creative concepts; and to remain true to their individual expressions. However, they are honing their art skills and techniques, and appreciate artwork whose results are pleasing and significant, yet uniquely their own.

Children will begin to discover their unique artistic independence, the mysteries of combining art mediums, the joy of exploration, the delight of creating something from nothing, and the wonder and pride in serious artistic challenges. Some of their artwork will have results that can be improved and refined in continual attempts and practice; other art experiences will astonish and astound them through one gigantic plunge; still other artwork will mystify them and lead them to deeper exploration, practice, and ultimate understanding.

Art is an exciting experience that encourages individuals to explore and discover their abilities and expressions, with artistic results that range from astonished to delighted, spectacular to breath-taking, lovely to reserved, charming to rare. And as the adults who help it all to take place, we are allowed the gift of seeing it happen before our very eyes.

About *Primary Art*

The activities in *Primary Art* are written for young artists ages 5 to 10 to experience at home, at school, in after-school programs, or anywhere children have the time, materials, and inclination to create. In *Primary Art*, the 150+ art experiences respect the individual's creativity, promote the process of art exploration, and significance of the resulting art. Each individual's artwork is expected to express his or her creativity, and not to reflect a pre-made sample or mock-up.

This book is organized in four chapters: Draw & Design (crayon, chalk, pencil, pen), Paint & Print (tempera, acrylic, watercolor, dye, ink), Collage & Assemble (cut-and-paste, mosaic, weave, and sew), and Sculpt & Construct (clay, dough, wire, wood, papier-mâché, and plaster of Paris).

The art experiences are presented in groups of three. First, within every set of experiences is "For the Budding Artist," which contains simple activities to help young artists become familiar with the materials and learn about the properties of different artistic mediums through beginning art experiences. The second part is called "Preliminary Art Experience," which is an introductory art experience; and the third part is the "Primary Art Experience," which builds on the skills of the previous two parts.

All projects have icons that tell, among other things, how long the project might take to set up, and if it is easy or challenging. All illustrations are designed to clarify the direction of the project, but not to give absolute expectations of how the project should look upon completion. The illustrations are only suggestions to help artists get started or clarify steps.

Artists are expected to assist in gathering supplies and materials, setting up, and cleaning up—all part of the reality of creativity!

For children of this age, art is an adventure!

About MaryAnn

MaryAnn Faubion Kohl is the author or co-author of many books of art experiences for children of all ages. Her company, Bright Ring Publishing Inc., (est. 1985) publishes *Storybook Art, Scribble Art, Mudworks, Mudworks Bilingual Edition, Good Earth Art, ScienceArts,* and *Discovering Great Artists.* She also writes books for Gryphon House, Inc. and is author or co-author of *Preschool Art, Cooking Art, Global Art, MathArts, Making Make-Believe, The Big Messy Art Book,*

and *First Art: Art Experiences for Toddlers and Twos.* MaryAnn's books have captured the imaginations of children, teachers, and parents all over the world.

MaryAnn's books have received the following awards:
2002 Gold, Art Appreciation, Practical Homeschooling Magazine
2001 Mayor's Art Award, Education and Support, Bellingham, Washington
2004 Director's Choice Award
1999 Gold Award, Best Parenting Book, National Parenting Publications
1999 Top Ten Award, The Education Source
1995 ALA Best of the Best Books and Media for Children
1993 Washington Press Communicator Award
Benjamin Franklin Gold and Silver Awards, for excellence in independent publishing

MaryAnn's background began as an elementary school teacher, and continued as a college educator and educational consultant. Currently, she is an author and publisher. Her interest in children's creative art comes from her years teaching preschool through middle school, teaching kindergarten enrichment and college-level courses, and consulting with teachers and parents throughout the world. MaryAnn says, "I love everything and anything creative with children, and art seems to be the thing I love best."

While a child growing up first in Longmeadow, Massachusetts, and later on Bainbridge Island, Washington, her favorite activities were art, music, reading, and especially playing outside. She says, "I treasured my box of pastel chalks, my Indian Princess bicycle, and my Ginny doll with her little trunk full of doll clothes. Now that I've grown up, I treasure my family! We live in Bellingham, Washington where my husband and I raised our two daughters. And I still enjoy playing outside! When I'm not writing or publishing, you'll find me kayaking, jetskiing, snow skiing, working in our woods, playing with our dog, reading, or best of all, enjoying some family fun. Consulting in the schools, offering workshops around the world, writing for magazines, and appearing on television keep me busy year round. But it's writing my books and spending time with children that make me happiest of all."

About the Icons

Each art activity is labeled with icons noting the project's needs such as experience level, planning and preparation required, time to complete the project, and if adult assistance is needed. The icons are suggestions, subject to personal and individual modifications and based on experience, needs, and readily available materials. Feel free to substitute materials, vary suggested techniques, or modify projects to suit abilities and preferences. Creative variation is part of the fun and success—and the process—of art with children. Expect completely unique results!

Experience Level—assists in choosing, not limiting, art experiences, with stars to indicate levels of ease.

Easy—Beginning (easy, few steps or materials, good for first experiences in art, and for artists of intermediate or high experience levels)

Moderate—Intermediate (more involved, combination of materials and steps, good for mid-level artists, or for beginning artists with assistance)

Involved—Experienced (complex or elaborate, more steps, more combinations of materials, good for experienced artists, or for less experienced artists with assistance)

Note: Age and experience do not necessarily go hand in hand. The experience icon flags projects according to levels from easy to complex. All artists can explore all projects: just remember that beginning artists may need assistance with mid- or high-level projects, while experienced artists enjoy the independence of easier projects.

Planning and Preparation—assists adults in choosing projects according to time needed for planning and preparation: assembling supplies and materials, setting up activities, cleaning up, and supervising artists.

easy   moderate   involved

Adult Assistance/Help/Caution—notes projects with supplies that may be sharp, hot, electrical, or need extra care and supervision. Adult help or assistance is required. Note those steps marked adult in bold type, which means that an adult only should perform the step, although a child may be allowed to assist.

Time to Complete the Art Project

1 hour or less   1 day or less   allow more than a day

Getting Ready!

Being prepared makes art more enjoyable for everyone. Here are some tips for exploring art with artists ages 5 to 10.

- **Art Space:** Many young artists work best standing or kneeling, often without chairs. A low table, or child-size table and chairs with feet touching the floor, reinforces success and comfort.
- **Drying Area:** A separate drying area protected with newspaper or other covering, where art projects may be left to dry undisturbed, helps keep art under control and safe, especially if several days for drying are required.
- **Laundry and Stains:** Paints and dyes do stain, but most will wash off skin after a bath or two and several shampoos. Keep spray laundry stain remover handy. (See The Cover-Up)
- **Recycle and Reuse:** It's never too late to start saving and collecting materials for art: collage items, fabric, paper scraps, Styrofoam grocery trays, yarn, sewing trims, junk mail, sticks, shells, beads, buttons, and pebbles. The list goes on! Wonderful and unusual recycled materials are available for free from local printers and frame shops: just bring a box! Yard sales and thrift stores offer inexpensive and inspiring materials for collage and sculpture. Ask friends and family to save specific items you need. Remember that doughs, clays, paste, and even some paints can be made instead of purchased.
- **Storing Materials:** Save heavy plastic bags, margarine tubs, yogurt cups, and shoeboxes for storing art materials. See-through plastic tubs with snap-on lids are an excellent choice for storing supplies. Shallow containers are often recommended in the project materials lists. These include cookie sheets with raised sides, baking pans, plastic trays, Styrofoam grocery trays, and plates.
- **Groups:** Working with children in small groups or individually encourages comfortable creativity and success more often than large-group involvement. When larger groups of children work together, enlist a volunteer or two to assist with replenishing art materials and carrying projects to drying areas. Older elementary-aged children, middle school children, and senior citizens are perfect choices for helpers with large-group art.

> *When my daughter was about seven years old, she asked me one day what I did at work. I told her I worked at the college—that my job was to teach people how to draw. She stared back at me, incredulous, and said, "You mean they forget?"*
>
> —Howard Ikemoto, artist/art teacher (1937)

Cover the Workspace

Cover the workspace or work surface with newspaper, whether it is a table, floor, chair, wall, or countertop. Tape the corners of paper to prevent wiggles and spills. It is easier to clean up by rolling spills and spots and sticky scraps into newspaper than to wash stained surfaces after the fact. Alternative covers recommended are flat sheets of cardboard, old shower curtains, vinyl picnic tablecloths, thin plastic party tablecloths, wide butcher paper or craft paper, or roll ends of newsprint from a local newspaper print shop. Children should help prepare surfaces so they have a better understanding of what protecting tables and floors is all about.

Handy Cleanup

Make cleanup easy and independent. Place a wet sponge or damp, small towel near projects to wipe hands as needed. Keep a bucket of warm soapy water near the workspace so children don't have to run to the sink. A few old towels for drying hands will keep nicer towels in good shape. A supply of damp rags and sponges are handy for wiping spills, tidying up, and cleaning splatters as needed.

The Cover-Up

Consider clothes that are worn for art only, offering worry-free creativity and exploration: slip on T-shirt, pull-on pants, old Velcro or slip-on sneakers (all of which become more unique with time and are often a source of pride). Other good cover-ups are an apron, a man's shirt with sleeves cut off, a smock, or a paint shirt. (A vinyl tablecloth can be cut into a smock that fits over a child's head and ties behind with strips of elastic sewn on the sides.)

Art Supplies & Materials

Purchasing and collecting art supplies ahead of time will encourage creativity and exploration with less stress and more spontaneity. Some basic supplies and special supplies are suggested in the following lists, as well as a list of collage materials.

Basic Supplies		Special Supplies		Collage Materials	
Aluminum foil, foil papers	Iron	Bamboo skewers	Liquid Watercolors™	Beads	Paper clips
Art tissue	Liquid starch	Brayer	Matte board	Bottle caps	Pebbles
Butcher paper, craft paper	Markers (permanent)	Camera, digital	Metal brads	Buttons	Pinecones
Cardboard	Marking pens (water based)	Cheesecloth	Metallic pens	Candy	Ping-pong balls
Chalk (pastels)	Masking tape	Embroidery thread	Papier-mâché	Checkers	Pipe cleaners
Collage items	Newsprint	Fabric	Photocopier	Cloves	Plastic lids
Colored pencils	Oil pastels	Fabric pens	Plaster cloth	Confetti	Popcorn
Construction paper	Paint: acrylic, tempera, watercolors	Fiberfill	Plaster of Paris	Corks	Rickrack
Contact paper	Paste	Fimo™, Sculpey™	Printing ink, water-soluble	Cotton balls	Rock salt
Craft sticks (popsicle sticks)	Pipe cleaners	Food coloring paste	Puffy pens	Easter grass	Rocks
Crayons	Playdough, play clay	Framing scraps	Sandwich baggies	Eggshells	Rubber bands
Drawing paper, white	Ribbon, raffia	Gesso	Shredded paper, confetti	Feathers	Sawdust
Fabric scraps	Scissors, quality/sharp	Glitter glue	Spray paint	Flowers	Sequins
Food coloring, liquid	Sequins	Glitter pens	Styrofoam block, sheet	Foam packing	Sponges
Glitter	Stapler	Glue, tacky	Twinkle lights	Gravel, fish tank	Spools
Glue, white (Elmer's Glue™)	Styrofoam grocery tray	Glue-gun	Wax paper	Gummed labels	Stars
Hammer, nails	Tape, transparent	Gouache	Wire	Hair rollers	Stickers
Homemade playdough	Warming tray	Hair gel	Wrapping paper	Hardware items	Straws
	Wiggle eyes	Hobby coating		Homemade playdough	String
	Yarn	Ink, water-based		Ice cream sticks	Tacks
				Jewelry pieces	Tees
				Junk items	Thistles
				Key rings	Tiles
				Keys	Tissue paper
				Lace	Toothpicks
				Leaves	Twigs
				Lids	Wallpaper
				Moss	Washers
				Nuts and bolts	Weeds
				Ornaments	Wood shavings
				Paint chips	Wool

1

Draw & Design

What art offers is space—a certain breathing room for the spirit.

—John Updike, novelist/writer (1932)

Penciled Watercolor

Paint directly on a sheet of heavy white drawing paper first moistened with a sponge.

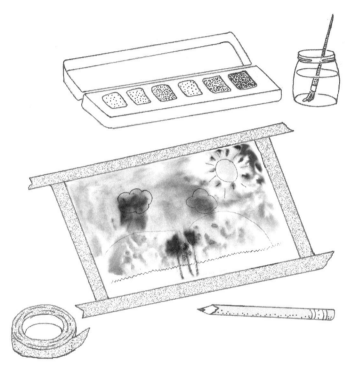

Materials

heavy white paper

masking tape

pencil (very soft drawing pencil works especially well)

sponge, wet

box of watercolor paints

paintbrush

jar of clean water

Process

1. Completely tape all four edges of a sheet of heavy white paper to the table. When peeled away, the tape will leave a natural framed border when the painting is complete.

2. Draw a picture with the pencil, adding many details and features.

3. Use a wet sponge to completely moisten the pencil drawing, but make sure that the paper is not too wet.

4. While the paper is wet, paint with watercolors over the pencil drawing. Paint freely and without constraint outside and over the pencil lines in any fashion. Rinse the brush often. The colors will blend, bleed, and blur. If the painting begins to dry, dip a paintbrush in a jar of clean water and moisten the paper.

5. Allow the drawing to dry completely. When dry, carefully and slowly peel the masking tape from the border, leaving a clean white frame around the pencil and watercolor artwork.

For Budding Artists

- Draw with colored water-based markers on plain paper first, and on wet paper next.
- Paint with watercolor paints on dry paper first, and wet paper next.

Pattern Design Blend

Trace a shape repeatedly on poster board to create an overlapping design. Draw patterns inside the shapes. Brush over the pattern design with water to blend and blur the colors.

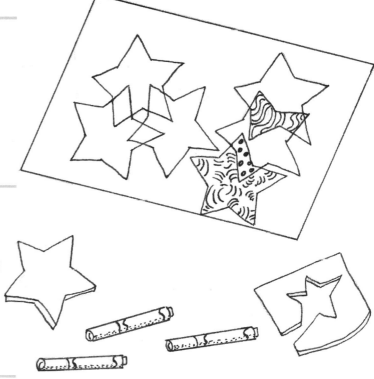

Materials

cardboard
scissors
colored markers, water-based (not permanent)
large piece of drawing paper or poster board
paintbrush
water

Process

1. Draw a shape on cardboard and cut it out.
2. Use colored markers to trace the shape numerous times on the drawing paper or poster board, overlapping the traced shapes.
3. Fill in the shapes with designs and patterns drawn with colored markers. Take special care to design within the areas made where shapes overlap.
4. Paint over the shapes and designs with water to mix, blur, and blend the colors.
5. When the drawing is dry, outline chosen areas with permanent black marker.

Variations

- Trace and overlap more than one shape within the same artwork.
- Brush designs with thin watercolor or food coloring instead of water.
- Sprinkle salt on the wet painting causing an exciting crystal-blur effect.

Spray & Scrape Resist

Spray a crayon drawing with thin paint. Scrape away the paint for a surprising crayon resist outcome.

Materials

pump spray bottle

tempera or watercolor paint*

water

crayons

heavy white paper

scraper, spatula, or other straight edge

> *Substitute food coloring mixed with water to a bright hue, or Liquid Watercolors™.

Process

1. Use water to thin tempera paints or watercolor paints.
2. Fill a pump bottle with the thinned paint.
3. Draw heavily and brightly with crayons on white paper. Bright waxy marks will work better than light thin marks.
4. Set the spray bottle to mist. Spray a light layer of paint on the crayon drawing. Immediately scrape the paint to one side with the straight edge. Add more paint to any areas that need paint and scrape it away again.
5. When satisfied with the results, allow the drawing to dry for a few minutes.

For Budding Artists

- Draw with crayons freely on plain paper.
- Spray water from a hand-misting bottle on a sidewalk or piece of cardboard.

3-D Impression

Spray a colored-marker drawing with a fine mist of water. Attach stand-out shapes in matching colors and designs to the first drawing, creating a misty impressionist artwork.

Materials

colored markers (water-based, not permanent)

heavy white drawing paper, 2 sheets

pump spray bottle

water

scissors

1"–2" (5cm) cardboard squares, approximately 20–30

white glue

Process

1. Fill a pump spray bottle with water. With a colored marker, draw three to five shapes on the paper. Draw the same matching three to five shapes on the second sheet of paper.

2. Within the outline of each shape, use the markers to draw patterns, such as circles, diamonds, squares, rectangles, triangles, squiggles, and ovals. Fill all the shapes with designs. Do the same on the second sheet of paper, repeating patterns, designs, and colors.

3. Spray a fine mist of water over the first completed drawing and let it dry. (Do nothing to the second drawing.) The water will bleed and blur the first drawing.

Hint: Holding the spray bottle about three feet from the drawing and misting lightly will allow the colors to blend into one another. Allow the wet drawing to dry undisturbed. (Brush gently across areas of the drawing with a wet brush to achieve a similar effect.)

4. While the first drawing dries, cut out each shape from the second drawing. To prepare the 3-D effect, glue several small squares of cardboard to the back of each shape. For a thicker 3-D look, stack three cardboard squares and glue them together (see illustration). Glue several small stacks to the backs of the shapes. Allow the glue to dry until strong.

5. When both drawings are dry, glue the cut-out shapes from the second drawing to the first sprayed drawing. Glue them anywhere within the design. The cut-out shapes will stand away from the second drawing, producing a 3-D impression.

Doodlectable Spectrum

Start from one small shape and draw ever-expanding doodle lines, changing colors at any time.

Materials

scissors

colored construction paper

choices of drawing tools, such as:

fine- or medium-tipped colored markers, black pencils, and colored pencils

glue or tape

Process

1. Cut a 6" x 6" (15cm x 15cm) square out of colored construction paper and a slightly larger square from another piece of colored construction paper. Begin a doodle in a corner or center of the smaller colored square by drawing a shape.

2. Follow that shape and make a line around it. Build another line around that shape.

3. Continue building lines and shapes, filling in areas that are blank with more lines and shapes.

4. Change pen color whenever desired.

5. There are no rules to doodling. However, if a rule sounds like fun, decide on one to follow throughout the doodle, such as:
   - No lines may touch other lines.
   - Whenever a shape changes, change the line color.
   - Change colors at the count of 10.
   - Alternate using thick and thin lines.

6. Fill the entire paper with the growing doodle. Take as long as needed. A doodle may last for several days before it is complete. When the doodle lines are complete, fill in some of the doodle spaces with colored pencil, if desired.

7. Glue the doodle square to a slightly larger square of construction paper for display.

For Budding Artists

- Draw pictures with pencil on plain paper.
- Draw freely with fine- or medium-tipped colored markers on plain paper.
- Glue paper scraps with white glue squeezed directly from the bottle.

Series Cartooning

Create an original cartoon comic strip in a series of three sections.

Materials

newspaper comic strips

choice of drawing tools, such as colored markers, crayons, colored pencils, black pen, ballpoint pen, pencil

extra drawing paper for practice

3 or more white paper squares, approximately 3½" (9cm) square

strip of drawing paper, 12" x 4" (30cm x 10cm)

scissors

glue or tape

Process

1. Look at comic strips in the newspaper. Think about a main character to invent for a new and original comic strip. It could be a person, an animal, or an imaginary creature. It could even be a car or a cloud! Practice creating and drawing the character. Explore drawing different positions or actions and facial expressions, such as happy, surprised, confused, or sleepy. Think of a name for the character of the comic.

2. Next, think of a short story that you can tell in three sequential steps. Most comics are funny, but they can be serious or instructional, too. Any story will do. Here are a few examples:
   - 1) Boy wakes up. 2) He walks to school. 3) He finds out it is Saturday and school is closed.
   - 1) Dog scares a cat. 2) Cat scares a mouse. 3) Mouse scares the dog.
   - 1) Seed is in the ground. 2) Seed sprouts. 3) Sprout blossoms into flower.

3. When the story idea is ready, draw the first part on a square of white paper. Draw the second part of the story on another square, and the final ending on a third square. Add words and voices in bubbles or print.

4. Fold the strip of drawing paper into thirds. Then unfold and flatten the strip.

5. Tape or glue all three squares in order on the strip. Write the name of the strip on one corner. Don't forget to sign the comic strip.

Magni-Draw

Choose an interesting small portion of a subject. Draw the small portion as if enlarged by a magnifying glass.

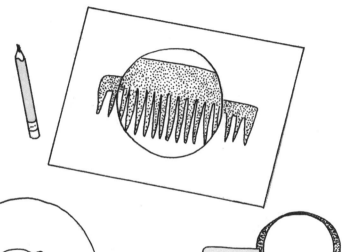

Materials

magnifying glass

colored pencils, colored markers, or crayons

large white drawing paper

scissors

pencil

choice of a circle template to trace, including:

    cooking pot lid, hula hoop, pizza cardboard circle, other circular items

Process

1. Find an object or subject of interest to draw, such as a leaf, flower, pet, shell, or other idea. Look at it through a magnifying glass to see the enlarged details.

2. Next, select only a portion of the subject to draw in magnified detail. For example, if looking at a whole flower, choose to draw only the magnified center of the blossom in detail. If looking at the family dog, choose to draw only the magnified eyes and nose in detail. Think of the drawing as a magnification of a part of the whole subject.

3. Draw the magnified portion of the subject on a large scale so that it fills the large paper. Include as many details as possible. Look carefully at the subject or object through a magnifying glass to capture as many details as possible.

4. When finished, trace a very large circle around the drawing, using a template suggested in the materials list above or another circular item. Cut around the circle outline. The paper circle will resemble only what is seen in a magnifying glass.

For Budding Artists

- Draw pictures with pencil, crayon, and markers on plain paper.
- Trace lids and patterns to make shapes.

Circle Peek-a-View

Peek through a cardboard tube and spot an interesting subject to draw. Notice how it fits within the circle. Visualize it and remember it. Draw the same image within a black line circle on drawing paper.

Materials

cardboard tube (or sheet of paper rolled into tube)

drawing paper

thick black marker

circle template (bowl, coffee can lid, or other round object)

colored pencils, colored markers or crayons

Process

1. Look through a cardboard tube or rolled-up paper, indoors or outdoors.
2. Spot something interesting and remember it as it looks within that circle.
3. Next, trace a large black circle in the center of a sheet of white paper (this is the frame of the "circle view").
4. Inside the circle boundaries, draw what was seen through the tube.

Circle Ideas

- Draw what is seen inside the circle view and also what is seen around it.
- Draw four circles on the paper to show views from one location looking North, South, East, and West.

Color Grid

Fill a small folded paper grid with chosen colors. Then create a matching larger grid with squares of colored paper.

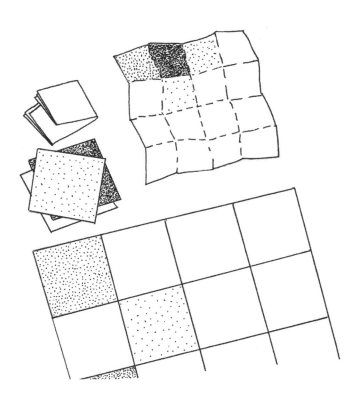

Materials

white copier paper	4″ (10 cm) squares of colored paper, 16 squares
colored pencils or crayons	scissors
white drawing paper	glue stick

Process

1. To make a grid from the copier paper: Cut the copier paper so that it is a square, about 8″ x 8″ (20cm x 20cm). Fold the square of copier paper into 16 sections (four sections by four sections). To do this, fold the paper in half four times, keeping the paper shape square—fold in half, fold in half again, again, and one last time. Press all edges sharply. Then unfold and spread out flat. The 16 sections should all be about 2″ (5cm) square.

2. Color in each square with any color desired. Use the fold lines as guides. Use no fewer than two colors, and no more than eight colors. When all the squares are colored in, set it aside.

3. To make the larger grid from drawing paper: Cut the paper into a 16″ x 16″ (40cm x 40cm) square. Fold the square of drawing paper into 16 sections, just as before. However, the squares will be 4″ (10cm), and the paper will be thicker and harder to fold. Press the edges sharply. Then unfold and spread out flat.

4. Now, create an exact copy of the smaller pencil-colored grid on the larger grid paper. To do this, cut squares of colored paper. Cut the paper into 4″ x 4″ (10cm) squares.

   Hint: Use the same colors of paper as the colors in the small grid.

5. Look at the small grid. If the square in the upper right-hand corner is red, glue a red paper square on the larger grid in the matching space. If a square in the middle is blue, glue a square of blue paper in the matching position on the larger grid. Continue until all the large grid squares are filled with colored paper squares.

Finishing Ideas

- **Small Grid**: with a ruler and black marker, draw black lines on the fold lines of the grid to create distinct boxes.
- **Large Grid**: Stretch narrow masking tape over the fold lines of the grid to make broad dividing lines and definite boxes. Another idea is to glue narrow, colored, 16″ (40cm) strips of paper over the fold lines.

For Budding Artists

- Draw lines with a ruler or straight edge on plain paper.
- Fold square paper into sections—halves, quarters, and more.

Simple Grid Enlargement

Make an enlargement of an original drawing using a simplified grid approach. This is a technique that artists use.

Materials

child's original drawing (simple, bold, few details)

scissors

pencil

ruler or yardstick

large sheet of white drawing paper (about double the size of the drawing)

crayons

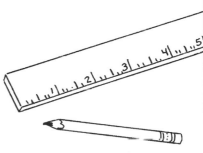

Process

1. Trim the child's drawing to a square shape (not a rectangle).

2. To make the grid: Fold the square drawing into 16 sections by folding the drawing in half four times. Fold it in half, in half again, in half again, and one last time. Then unfold. Sixteen sections should show, four by four. With a ruler or yardstick, draw a straight pencil line along each fold line to make a grid. Set aside.

3. To make the enlarged grid: With adult help, draw 16 equal sections, four by four, on a larger sheet of paper, at least double the size of the smaller grid sections. For example, if the original sections are 2" (5cm) wide, the larger sections should be at least 4" (10cm) wide or larger (see illustration).

4. Look at the first section of the drawing with the pencil line grid. Draw the same lines in the enlarged grid (see illustration) in the first section, but draw them larger to fit the section. Do this for each grid section, one at a time. Soon all the sections will come together to form one enlarged copy of the original.

5. Color the enlarged drawing to match the original.

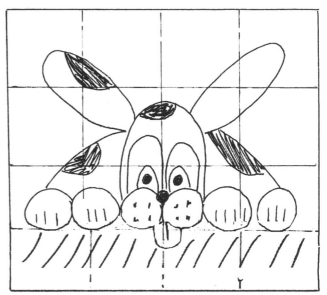

Copy That Transfer

Make a traced transfer to capture the main elements of a magazine picture.

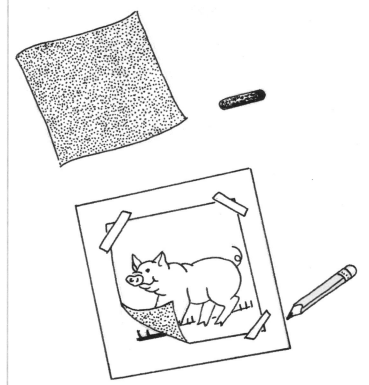

Materials

magazine picture
scissors
crayon or colored chalk
drawing paper
tape
soft pencil
colored pencil

Process

1. Find an interesting bold and simple picture in a magazine and cut it out.
2. Color on the back of the picture with crayon or colored chalk. Work carefully as magazine paper tends to tear. (Repair tears with tape, if needed.)
3. Place the magazine picture crayon side down on a sheet of drawing paper, and tape both the drawing paper and all four corners of the magazine picture to the table to hold them in place.
4. Trace lines in the magazine picture with a soft pencil, using firm pressure and moving slowly. (Peek under the magazine picture to see the lines transfer onto the drawing paper.)
5. When ready, peel off the taped corners to see the transfer.
6. Color the transferred drawing with colored pencils to match the original magazine picture, or select different colors. Display the magazine picture alongside the new transfer, if desired.

For Budding Artists

- Cut pictures from magazines and glue on plain paper.

Half 'n Half Art

Draw the missing half of a magazine picture. The results are amazing!

Materials

magazines

scissors

glue stick

drawing paper

colored pencils and fine point markers

Process

1. Cut out an interesting bold and simple picture from an old magazine. Especially successful subjects are people's faces, animals, flowers, and scenery.
2. Cut the picture in half.
3. Glue one half of the picture to the drawing paper. Let dry.
4. Use colored pencils and pens to draw the connected missing half of the picture in the blank spaces.

Missing Parts Ideas

- Share the other half of the magazine picture with a friend. Both artists complete the missing half in a drawing, and see how the resulting drawings compare.
- Glue a whole picture in the center of a larger piece of drawing paper. Add in the parts of the picture that are not seen. For example, draw the arms and legs of a person that are left out, or parts of the background that are missing.

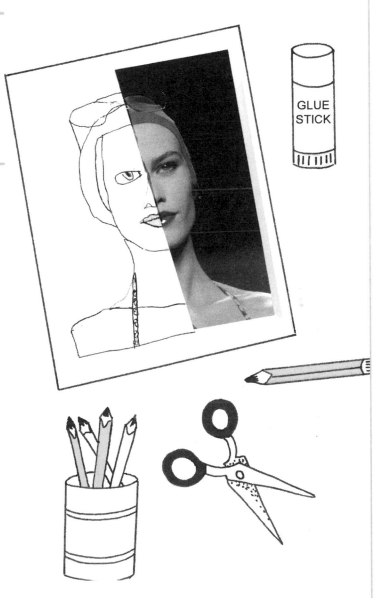

Color Wheel Exercise

The color wheel shows colors that are complementary, that is, colors that are found opposite each other on the wheel and that work well together. Choose two complementary colors and create a drawing using these two colors only.

Materials

color wheel (found in art books, art stores, and on the Internet)

white drawing paper, 9" x 12" (24cm x 30cm)

colored paper, 12" x 18" (30cm x 45cm)

two complementary color crayons (choose two complementary colors from the color wheel)

tape, glue, or stapler

Process

1. Look at a color wheel. See how the complementary colors are those that are opposite on the wheel. Find complementary color pairs, such as red and green, blue and orange, or yellow and purple. When used together, complementary colors each make the other look vibrant and bright.

2. Choose two complementary colors and select crayons of the same colors to make a drawing. Draw any simple picture such as a self-portrait or the family pet sleeping on the rug. Keep details to a minimum. Use only complementary colors. For interest, color some areas lightly and other areas hard and bright. Fill in the background with a pattern or texture. Use heavy lines and light lines, heavy coloring and light coloring.

3. Mount the drawing on a larger piece of colored paper in one of the complementary colors. If the color is not available, use white or black.

Hint: For fun, stare at the completed drawing, and then, quickly avert eyes to a blank white wall or white sheet of paper. Sometimes complementary colors can play a trick on the eyes so the drawn image seems to appear on white.

For Budding Artists

- Look at an object and draw it in detail on paper.

Drawing for Exercise

Make a contour drawing by looking at the subject but not looking at the drawing hand. This drawing experience is a way to exercise the eye to draw what it sees, not what it thinks it sees. As with any form of exercise, the more one does it, the better the results.

Materials

pencil

paper

common objects, such as:

    a book, chair, hand, plant, shell, or shoe

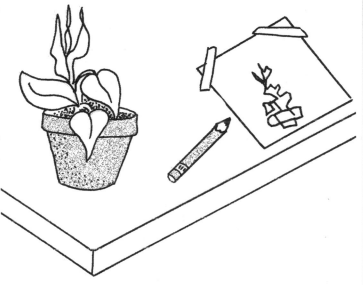

Process

1. Choose an object to draw. Relax and sit comfortably with a pencil in the drawing hand, resting on the drawing paper.

2. Find a starting point on the object where the eye can start looking at the outer edge of the object. This is called the contour. Let the eye exercise itself by slowly following the line of the object.

3. Meanwhile, let the pencil move as the eye moves. Draw the contour of the object without lifting the pencil from the drawing. Most importantly, do not look at the drawing. If peeking occurs, place the drawing paper inside a box with a hole for the drawing hand. Draw inside the box so that peeking is prevented.

4. When the contour is finished, look at the drawing. Does it look like the object? Usually, the first time a contour drawing is done it will not look like the object. As with all exercise, keep repeating the exercise over and over. Practice will bring the reward of better and better contour drawings.

Scribble Dabble

Stick masking tape in a design on paper, and scribble over the paper and tape with crayons or markers. When finished, remove the tape to see the remaining design.

Materials

masking tape

choice of construction paper (any color, including white)

crayons or colored markers

Process

1. Stick strips of masking tape to a sheet of construction paper in any design. Stick the tape lightly to make it easier to remove later.
2. Scribble vigorously over the entire paper and tape, changing colors frequently.
3. When the paper is filled with color, carefully and slowly peel the masking tape away revealing the remaining design.

For Budding Artists

- Peel masking tape from a roll and tear it off. Stick it to paper.

Peel-Away Tape Design

Stick masking tape on a piece of matte board, embellish the open spaces with color, and then peel away the tape for a final design.

Materials

square of white matte board

masking tape (blue painter's masking tape works well)

crayons

paint

colored markers

scissors

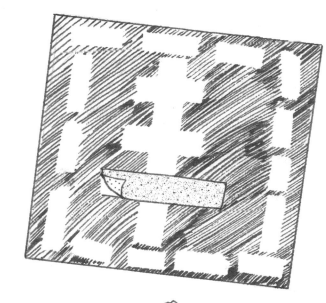

Process

1. Stick strips of masking tape to a square of matte board in a planned design. Use design features and techniques by crossing the tape over itself, overlapping strips, and tearing off small pieces to stick to the design. It is important to plan to leave areas of white matte board showing between tape pieces.

2. Color the spaces left between the tape lines with crayons, paint, or colored markers. The colors may be solid, or patterns and designs may be drawn to fill in the spaces.

3. Carefully and slowly peel away the tape to see the stencil effect remaining on the matte board. (Tape may be left on the work instead, if preferred.)

Other Tape and Stencil Ideas

- Spray the masking tape design with thinned tempera paint or liquid watercolor paint. Then remove the masking tape.

- Use contact paper instead of tape. Peel away after coloring the spaces and areas outside the contact paper.

- Tape designs on a blank T-shirt. Color in the open spaces with fabric marker. Then peel off the tape.

Handy Design

Fill in a tracing of one's own hand with fancy patterns and designs.

Materials

paper, any color
choice of coloring tools, such as:
    crayons, pens, colored chalk, oil pastels, or paint pens
scissors
glue

Process

1. Trace one's own hand on paper.
2. Fill in the traced shape with drawings, designs, and colors.
3. Cut out the finished hand shape.
4. Glue the hand shape on a piece of construction paper.

Another Idea

- Trace and cut hand shapes in different colors. Arrange and overlap into the handy design.

For Budding Artists

- Make hand shadows on the wall.
- Trace around the shadow of any object cast on a piece of paper.
- Color a simple outlined drawing or coloring book page.
- Cut out a simple shape and glue it on paper.

Opti-ette

Black paper silhouettes are colored in with bright designs to create an optical extravaganza.

Materials

three sheets of colored paper

    1.) one sheet of white, black or other color

    2.) one sheet of a contrasting or matching color

    3.) one larger black sheet for a frame

white chalk or pencil

colored chalk or oil pastels

scissors

glue or tape

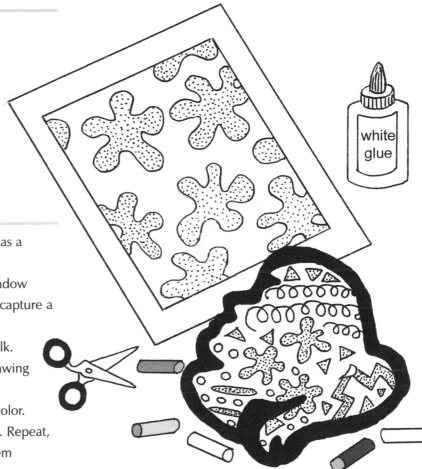

Process

1. Create a silhouette of any chosen subject on (1) the first sheet of paper, such as a human profile, animal body, tree, flower, boat, or other idea.

Hint: It works well to tape paper to the wall and use a bright light to cast the shadow of an object on that paper. Then trace the shadow with white chalk or pencil to capture a silhouette.

2. Fill the shape with bright designs and patterns using oil pastels or colored chalk.

3. Cut out the shape, leaving a black paper border around it. Place it on the drawing table.

4. Select (2) a second sheet of construction paper in a matching or contrasting color.

5. Look at the silhouette and note some designs or drawings that are interesting. Repeat, drawing those same designs and patterns on the colored paper, but make them larger—even double the size. Fill the paper as desired.

6. When ready, glue the cut-out shape on the newly decorated colored paper.

7. Glue or tape the artwork on (3) a larger sheet of black construction paper so that a black border is visible around the entire artwork.

Puffy Stained Glass

Brush colored tissue paper pieces with thinned glue on wax paper. When dry, draw around shapes with black or metallic puffy paint to resemble stained glass.

Materials

glue, water, container

wax paper

colored tissue paper

paintbrush

black or metallic puffy paint

hole punch

yarn

Process

1. In a container, thin glue with water. Stir with a paintbrush.
2. Tear off a square of wax paper that is the approximate desired size of the final "stained glass."
3. Cut and tear tissue into interesting shapes of different sizes.
4. Paint down pieces of tissue to the wax paper with a paintbrush dipped in the thinned glue. Create a colorful stained glass-like pattern. The pieces of tissue can overlap to create variations in color and thickness.
5. When dry, squeeze metallic puffy paint over the tissue paper to connect shapes.
6. Choose to leave the stained glass art as is, or make a border with puffy paint. The border can be in a circle, diamond, or window-like shape. Dry.
7. Trim the stained glass design around the puffy paint border. Punch a hole in the top and hang it in a window.

For Budding Artists

- Paint liquid starch or thinned white glue onto paper and press tissue scraps into the starch or glue.
- Explore drawing with markers on paper, aluminum foil, and plastic wrap.

Shiny Foil Depiction

Draw with permanent markers on plastic wrap over foil, producing a stained glass look.

Materials

permanent markers, variety of colors
white paper
paper plate (strong, dinner-size)
aluminum foil
clear plastic wrap
masking tape
stapler
colored construction paper or matte board, 12" x 12" (30cm x 30cm)
glue

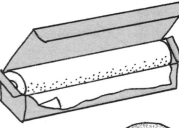

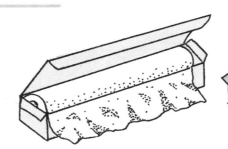

Process

1. Create an original drawing template: draw a simple, bold, black outline on white paper, similar to a coloring book illustration. If desired, create holiday symbol outlines, such as a Christmas tree, bell, angel, dreidel, menorah, star, heart, flag, snowflake, shamrock, or any other idea.

2. Cover a thick, dinner-size paper plate with aluminum foil. Set aside.

3. Place the drawing template on the table. Tape a sheet of clear plastic wrap over the template. Color in the drawing with permanent markers directly on the plastic wrap, filling in the outline.

4. Peel the plastic wrap from the template, and carefully stretch the colored plastic wrap over the foil-covered plate. Secure it tightly with masking tape to the back of the plate. Then staple the plastic wrap to the plate to hold securely.

5. Mount the plate on a square of construction paper or matte board with glue.

Transparent Art

Draw with permanent markers on clear plastic stretched over a sheet of white paper. Then peel away and tape in a window to see a colorful transformation.

Materials

sheet of white drawing paper
clear tape
clear plastic wrap
permanent markers
window

Process

1. Place a sheet of white paper on the table and tape the corners to hold it in place.
2. An adult should pull enough clear plastic wrap from the roll to cover the white paper. Tape it down to hold it in place.
3. Gently draw and color on the clear plastic with permanent colored markers. Fill the page with color.
4. When finished, an adult can help remove the tape and lift the plastic from the table.
5. Use clear plastic tape to attach the plastic wrap to a window. See how different the colors look without the white background, and with the sun or bright light shining through the color.

For Budding Artists

- Draw with markers on slick surfaces such as glass, clear plastic wrap, or plastic of any kind.

Translucent Window Gallery

Create translucent images from magazine clippings and contact paper.

Materials

clear contact paper	window (or a sheet of Plexiglas)
magazine picture (select pictures with bright contrasts of color, line, and shape)	transparent tape
	scissors
	pencil
spoon or ruler	permanent colored markers
tub of water	construction paper or poster board

Process

1. To make a translucent image: Cut a piece of clear contact paper into a square. Remove the backing and press the square onto a thin paper magazine image. Pictures with bright contrasts of color, line and shape work best.

2. Totally burnish the contact paper by rubbing it with a spoon or ruler so it becomes clear and adheres well to the picture. Place the square in a tub of water for at least 30 minutes. The adhesive of the contact paper will "lift off" the ink from the magazine picture and keep its image. Under gently running water, gently rub off any remaining "paper fuzz."

3. With a pencil, lightly trace the outside edge of the contact paper on drawing paper to acquire its shape and size for a frame. Remove the image. With colored markers (and a ruler, if needed), design a fancy frame on construction paper or poster board to go around the image. Choose to design a frame in any style, such as ornate, bold, simple, or modern. Cut out the frame, including the hole in the middle of the frame. Place the frame over the image. Tape it in place on the back of both the image and frame.

4. Tape the entire translucent image with its frame in a window or on a sheet of Plexiglas. Tape all four sides. Let the light shine through!

5. Make as many translucent framed images as desired. Create an entire window gallery!

Definition: Translucent means that light can shine through, but it is not completely clear or see-through. Embellish with drawn frames.

Variation

- In place of magazine pictures, substitute gift wrap, a road map, or any other paper image.

Be There and Be Square

Fold a paper in four or more sections. Draw a simple bold subject on the paper. When coloring it in, change color whenever the crayon crosses a line.

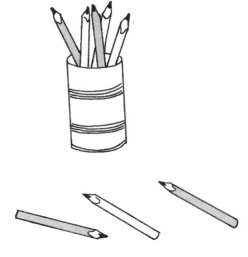

Materials

drawing paper

colored pens and pencils

Process

1. Fold a piece of drawing paper into four or more squares.
2. Unfold the paper and flatten it out.
3. Draw a bold and simple picture to fill the paper, crossing the folds or squares.
4. Color the drawing in, but wherever the picture crosses a fold line, change colors.
5. Fill in all of the squares with color, changing colors each time a line is crossed.

For Budding Artists

- Draw a squiggle that loops and overlaps on plain paper. Color in each section of the squiggle.

Be Wiggly and Be Squiggly

Create a drawing dissected by wiggly lines and changing colors.

Materials

pencil

sheet of drawing paper

choice of drawing tools, such as:

       chalk

       colored markers

       colored pencils

       crayons

       oil pastels

cotton ball, make-up pad, or facial tissue (optional)

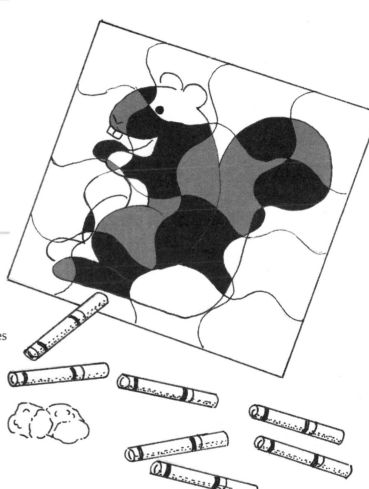

Process

1. With a pencil, lightly draw a "wiggly line" grid on the paper (see illustration). A grid is like a checkerboard with lines crossing and making many sections.

2. Draw a simple picture with few details that fills the drawing paper. The drawing will cross over the wiggly lines.

3. Choose a crayon or other tool for coloring the drawing, or mix several coloring choices at once. Colors can be wild or calm, bright or soft, scribbled or solid. Combining oil pastels and crayons creates an interesting effect.

4. Color the drawing, section by section. Each time a line is crossed, change colors.

Optional: When the coloring is complete, try rubbing the drawing vigorously with a cotton ball or make-up pad to shine and blend the colors.

Chalk Walk

Create a chalk artwork in a section of sidewalk for all to see.

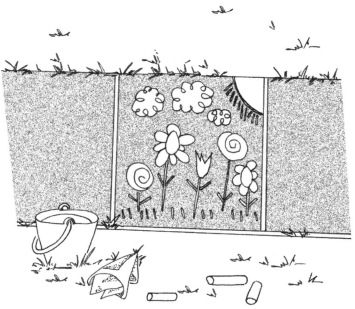

Materials

large sidewalk chalk 1" x 4" size (3cm x 10cm), variety of colors (available in craft stores, discount stores, school supply stores, and grocery stores)

plastic bag

sidewalk or playground

sponge and bucket of water for erasing and blending

Process

1. Fill a plastic bag with sidewalk chalk. Tie the bag to a belt or pocket so it is convenient for retrieving and dropping in chalk. Go for a "chalk walk" and find an area for creating chalk art.

2. With permission, select a square section of sidewalk for the drawing area. Begin by outlining the square. (If a sidewalk is not available, section off a square of playground or driveway about 4' x 4' [4m x 4m].)

3. Lightly sketch a large uncomplicated drawing in the square.

4. Fill in the drawing with colored chalk. Use a dry sponge to blend colors. Add a little water to the sponge to erase or blend colors further. Fill the entire sidewalk square with color.

5. When the chalk art is complete, inspect the drawing from all four sides, walking around the square to see different perspectives.

6. If more than one artist is working on the sidewalk or playground, go for a "chalk walk" when everyone has finished and view the results. Observe four perspectives for each drawing—top, bottom, right side, and left side.

Hint: Rain and footsteps will gradually erase the chalk art, so take a picture before it disappears!

For Budding Artists

- Draw with chalk on a sidewalk or playground.
- Draw with chalk on paper.

Glue Line Chalk

Glue lines create a border for a drawing that is filled with bright pastel chalk.

Materials

12″ x 18″ (30cm x 45cm) sheet of black construction paper

pencil

white glue in squeeze bottle

colored markers

pastel chalk, variety of colors

water

sugar

black light (optional)

Process

1. Draw a large shape on the black paper with a pencil.
2. Squeeze white glue over the pencil lines.
3. Dry overnight or longer, until hard and clear.
4. Color the dry glue lines with colored markers, or leave clear.
5. Color the spaces in the drawing with colored pastel chalks. Blend the lines with a tissue or cotton ball, if desired. For extra bright chalk, dip chalk in a sugar-water mixture and draw with damp chalk.
6. If available, shine a "black light" on the chalk drawing for an exciting visual experience.

My White Glue

Tempera Chalk Drawing

Explore mixing art mediums. Dip colored chalk into white tempera paint and draw on colored paper.

Materials

colored paper (any chosen color, including black)
masking tape
colored chalk
white tempera paint
cup
sponge or facial tissue
clear plastic wrap
tape

Process

1. With masking tape, make a 2" (5cm) border around all four edges of the colored paper, taping it to the table.
2. Pour white tempera paint into a cup. Dip the tip of the chalk into the white paint and draw shapes, designs, and patterns. Draw over the edges of the masking tape, too. The drawing will appear in bright color, edged with white. When the drawing dries, the chalk will be less smudgy than chalk used alone.
3. If desired, brush some of the chalk-paint with a sponge or tissue to blend the colors. Brush right over the masking tape.
4. When the drawing is finished, carefully and slowly peel the masking tape from the paper. A clean paper frame will remain.
5. If desired, cover the art with a large piece of clear plastic wrap. Tape it around to the back of the paper so the front looks shiny (like glass) and the chalk is protected.

For Budding Artists

- Dip chalk in water or sugar-water and draw on paper.
- Draw with chalk on wet paper.

It's a PIPP! (Pencil, Ink, Paint, Pastel)

PIPP is just another name for "mixed media drawing" with results that please young artists every time.

Materials

still-life (example: dried flowers arranged in a vase on a patterned tablecloth)	watercolor brushes
	bamboo skewers or wooden kabob sticks
pencil	drawing ink (waterproof is best)
watercolor paper (or heavy drawing paper that won't soak through)	watercolor paint
	pastel chalk
water in a container	cardboard

Process

1. Arrange a still life on the work table. Any subject will do, such as a bowl of fruit, vase of flowers, or basket of shells. Display on a patterned cloth for added interest. If preferred, draw a subject from the imagination, or look outdoors for inspiration.

2. Draw the basic outline of the still-life on a large sheet of watercolor paper or heavy drawing paper with light pencil. Details are not needed. Try to expand the still-life subject to fill the paper, rather than a tiny still-life in the center of the paper.

3. Moisten the paper with water from a clean paintbrush. The paper should be wet, but not soaked for Step 4.

4. **Ink Step** (dress appropriately—ink does not wash out): Dip the bamboo skewer into the waterproof ink. Go over the pencil lines with the ink. The ink will make blips and blobs, part of the artistic effect. When all tracing is done, let the ink dry for about 30 minutes.

5. **Watercolor Paint Step**: Next, add more details and color with wet watercolor paint and a small brush. Use enough water to get the paint flowing.

6. **Pastel Chalk Step**: Highlight or touch certain areas of the painting with chalk. A little chalk is all that is needed.

7. Allow the art to dry. Mount on cardboard by folding a small border of the artwork around the cardboard and taping the edges on the back.

Clipped Inset Drawing

Incorporate a magazine clipping into the essential elements of a drawing.

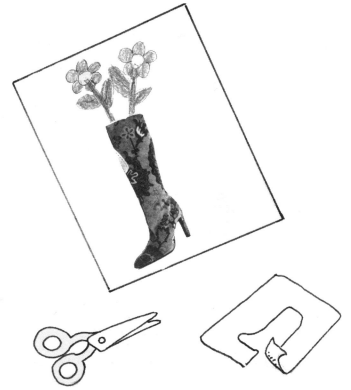

Materials

catalogs and magazines

scissors

glue stick

drawing paper

choice of drawing tools, such as colored markers, colored pencils, and crayons

scrap paper

Process

1. Select pictures from magazines or catalogs. Tear or cut out the pictures.
   Hint: Choose pictures with clear, uncluttered images. Adults can pre-select pictures and place them in a box, or artists can discover their own.
2. Glue the picture on the drawing paper. For example, cut out a woman's smiling face and glue this on the drawing paper. (See illustration for boot example.)
3. Draw a picture incorporating the clipped magazine image into a drawing in an imaginative way. For example, a smiling face could be:
   - the face on a clock
   - blended into a puffy cloud
   - peeking out of a castle tower
   - a new planet in the solar system

Suggestions and Ideas

- Cut out pictures of coins and glue on a drawing to represent flower blossoms in a vase.
- Cut out a picture of a horse and draw wings to create a flying horse like Pegasus.
- Cut out a dog and draw an umbrella for it to hold in its mouth.
- Change a cutout flower into a fantasy bird with wings and eyes.

Hint: More than one cutout may be used in a drawing.

For Budding Artists

- Glue magazine pictures to plain paper.
- Make a picture out of a squiggle that is pre-drawn on paper.

Surreal Clipping

Incorporate enlarged and reduced copies of a magazine picture into a surreal drawing composition.

Materials

catalogs and magazines

scissors

photocopy machine

drawing paper

glue stick

choice of drawing tools, such as colored markers, colored pencils, and crayons

Process

1. Select one interesting image from a magazine or catalog. Tear or cut out the image.
Hint: Choose a picture clipping that inspires the imagination.

2. Place the clipped image on a photocopier, and reproduce several enlarged images and several reduced images. Experiment with different sizes of reproduction. Save them all for the next step.

3. Cut out a selection of images in different sizes. Arrange them on the drawing paper while imagining how they might work together in one picture. For example, a flower enlarged and reduced many times might become a garden full of dancing flowers, both grown-up flowers and baby flowers. Or reproductions of a lion in different sizes might become a basket full of lion kittens with a large mother and father lion.

4. When an idea is forming, create a drawing that incorporates the cutout images. Draw details and features to add to the drawing. (Begin with either drawing or with gluing.)
Hint: Use minimal glue to prevent glue from smearing on the drawing.

Name Flame

Create a red-hot flaming design using a name as the underlying basis.

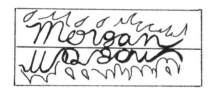

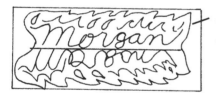

Cut out, then paste on background paper

Materials

white drawing paper, 8½" x 11" (20cm x 30cm)
pencil
1 stick of blue or colored chalk
spoon, ruler, or wooden craft stick
wide or heavy-tipped black marker

crayons in flaming colors (shades of orange, red, yellow, blue)
soft cloth (or facial tissue)
scissors
glue stick
black paper, 8½" x 11" (20cm x 30cm)

Process

1. Fold the paper in half lengthwise (the long way), matching the corners. Then press the folded edge and crease. Open. Flatten the paper on the table with the fold running from left to right (the long way).

2. Print or write a name with pencil on the folded line in the top half of the paper. Draw the letters in a design large enough to almost fill the top half of the paper. Cursive writing has the most flame-like design, but printing will work fine.

3. To transfer the letters to the other half of the paper, trace the pencil letters heavily with blue or colored chalk. Then refold the paper so the letters and chalk are inside the fold. Rub the outside of the paper with the back of a spoon, a ruler, or a wooden craft stick. Peek inside the folded paper and see if the letters have transferred to the other side of the folded paper. Continue rubbing until they are well transferred. Then open again.

4. Trace all the letters, both pencil and chalk lines, with a wide black marker. Excess chalk may be brushed away with a tissue or soft cloth.

5. To turn the name design into flames, color in the spaces with flaming colors such as red, orange, yellow, and blue (blue is the hottest part of the flame). Draw pointed flame shapes stretching out from the design in different flame colors. Try mixing more than one crayon color within the shapes. Color bright and heavy to make the colors shine. Rub the flames with a soft cloth to polish them to a shiny end result.

6. Cut around the entire flaming name (see illustration) with a wavy or pointy technique. Glue the name flame to a black background paper and display.

For Budding Artists

- Print a name or word on paper, and then color and decorate it with crayon.

Illuminated Manuscript

Decorate a letter of the alphabet with flourishing ornate designs and highlight with metallic pens.

Materials

books about medieval times containing decorative gold lettering

pencil

white drawing paper, 8½" x 11" (20cm x 30cm)

colored pencils

colored markers (optional)

metallic pens and pencils

foil paper, foil wrapping paper, or aluminum foil

scissors

second sheet of paper, larger than first

glue stick

Process

Getting Ready: Looking at Illuminated Manuscripts

- Look at pictures of books from medieval times with highly decorative gold lettering called illuminated manuscript. The first letter on the first page of the book is larger than the rest, and is illustrated with gold and fancy decorations and details. The Internet is a great resource to see illuminated manuscripts in detail and color, or browse library shelves for examples of illuminated manuscripts in books.

Creating an Illuminated Manuscript

1. Think about a letter of the alphabet to transform into an illuminated manuscript (first letter of a name, any favorite shaped letter, or first letter of a poem or story).
2. Lightly sketch the basic shape of the chosen letter on white drawing paper, filling the center of the paper with the large letter.
3. Increase the width of the letter's lines to at least 1" (5 cm) or wider. Lightly sketch fancy flourishes and decorations to make the letter's shape more ornamental. Add other decorative ideas to the illumination, such as birds, vines, flowers, and scrolls.
4. When the pencil sketch is complete, color the work with colored pencils. Color softly to fill large spaces. Add more color with markers, if desired.
5. With metallic pens or pencils, add gold or silver highlights to the letter to make it truly illuminated. Foil paper may also be cut to fit in selected spaces. Glue with a glue stick.
6. Mount the finished illuminated manuscript on a larger sheet of paper to give it a border and set off the finished work. Further designs may be added to the border to resemble a fancy frame.

Sprinkled Glue Drawing

Draw with squeezed white glue. Then press the drawing into confetti or other fun sprinkles.

Materials

shallow trays	choice of "sprinkles," such as:	crushed autumn leaves
pencil	candy sprinkles	crushed colored chalk
white glue in squeeze bottle	chopped crinkled paper	glitter
white poster board or	chopped Easter grass	paper punch dots
matte board	cinnamon, nutmeg, spices	sawdust
	colored sand	wood shavings
	confetti	

Process

1. Fill a shallow tray with a choice of art sprinkles. One tray of sprinkles is enough for beginners working with glue drawing. Two or three sprinkle choices will add to the experience.
2. With a pencil, lightly draw a simple design without details on the matte board. A few ideas for designs are:
   - abstract designs
   - flowers
   - geometric shapes
   - holiday symbols
   - squiggles and dots
   - words or names
3. Trace over all the pencil lines with white glue squeezed from the bottle. Thick lines work best. Keep in mind glue may spread out and bump into other lines.
4. Carefully and quickly turn the matte board over, and keeping it flat, press it into the sprinkles in the tray. The glue drawing will flatten somewhat as it picks up the sprinkles.
5. Lift the matte board, and turn it to the original side. Let the glue drawing dry on a flat surface overnight. The outcome will be crispy, clear, and sprinkly.

Hint: Instead of pressing the design into sprinkles, pinches of different sprinkles can be pressed or dropped onto the glue drawing wherever color and texture is preferred.

For Budding Artists

- Squeeze white glue on paper. Sprinkle confetti or paper punch holes in the glue.

Washaway Draw & Paint

Draw a simple picture with squeezed white glue. When dry, paint over the drawing, and then, wash the paint away with water.

Materials

pencil

drawing paper

white glue in squeeze bottle

white drawing paper

tempera paint, onc color

paintbrush

tub of water (or sink)

small sponge

choice of additional coloring materials, such as:

crayons, oil pastels, paintbrushes, and tempera paints

Process

1. With a pencil, lightly draw a simple picture without details. The picture will be like an outline, similar to a picture from a coloring book.

2. Trace over the pencil lines with white glue squeezed from the bottle. Thick lines work best. Then let the glue dry, usually overnight or over a weekend.

3. Paint over the entire paper with tempera paint. Set aside until completely dry.

4. Gently dip the entire artwork into a tub of water. Use the small sponge to loosen paint. The paint will quickly dilute into light and dark shades.

5. Let the painting dry on a pad of newspaper.

6. When the painting is dry, highlight the painting with crayon, oil pastels, or additional tempera paints.

Photocopy Repeat

Choose a portrait photo or any photograph with a simple subject. Copy and enlarge the photo nine times. Assemble the enlargements edge to edge on poster board. Embellish each copy in a different way.

Materials

portrait photo, or any single subject photo
photocopier with enlargement feature
large piece of poster board
glue
markers
crayons

Process

1. Copy a chosen photograph in black and white. Make nine copies enlarged to approximately a full sheet of copier paper.
2. On a larger piece of poster board, glue the nine copies edge to edge, three across and three down. Let the glue dry before proceeding to step 3.

Hint: Choose to glue several photographs upside down.

3. Each of the nine squares will be colored and decorated in a different way.

Suggestions
- add a variety of hair colors
- add patterns and designs to the clothing
- add a variety of hats
- add facial features, glasses, beard, earrings
- change the background colors
- change the skin colors

For Budding Artists

- Make a photocopy of an image.
- Enlarge and reduce the image.

Posed Imitation

Photocopy and enlarge a posed photo to imitate the main character from a famous painting or artwork. Then color the imitation work to look like the original masterpiece.

Materials

camera
photocopier
enlarged copy of photograph
scissors
glue stick
drawing paper
crayons, markers, colored pencils
framing matte or old picture frame

Process

1. Look at portrait masterpieces in books, from old art calendars, or on the Internet. Some portrait masters particularly suitable for this activity are: Rembrandt, Rubens, Raphael, Michelangelo, Warhol, and Kahlo. Keep a copy of the portrait masterpiece handy during this project. Print one from the Internet, or keep a book or calendar version handy.

2. Pose for a photograph in the same position and with the same expression as the person in the chosen famous masterpiece.

3. When the picture is printed, enlarge it on a photocopier or the computer to fit on a sheet of drawing paper with room for details around it. Cut out just the face, or cut out the entire body shape. Glue it to the drawing paper using a minimum amount of glue. The glue should be dry before beginning the next step.

4. Changing the photograph into the main subject of the masterpiece requires looking at the original masterpiece and noticing details. Color details and features to resemble the original masterpiece, such as background scenery, hair, hat, props, and costumes (see illustration).

5. Frame the imitation portrait in an old picture frame like a true masterpiece. A framing matte would also be an easy and effective frame.

Mini Master

Create a tiny work of art on a blank slide. Decorate the slide mount with sequins and metallic markers.

Materials

blank slides, 2" (5cm) (from any photography supply store or variety store)

embellishing materials, such as:

- beads
- confetti
- fishing line
- foil bits
- glitter
- glue
- gold thread
- hole punches
- metallic pens
- pushpins
- sequins
- fine-point markers, permanent (black, variety of colors)

Process

1. Draw a teeny tiny artwork on the blank film slide with fine-point permanent markers. Draw on the slide mount (the frame) too.
2. Decorate the slide mount with metallic pens, hole punches, or other embellishments.
3. String a fishing line or other thread through the slide mount. Hang from a pushpin in the ceiling, from a window, or on the wall.

Hint: Displaying many mini-masters makes a mini-gallery!

For Budding Artists

- Draw with markers on clear plastic or foil.
- Dress in costumes to imitate characters in favorite picture books.

Master of Parody

A parody is a work that imitates another artist's style, often in a humorous way. Using a portion of a fine art print, create a new work of art that is a parody.

Materials

fine art print of a figure or person (from the Renaissance or other long-ago era) (about 4" x 6" [10cm-15cm] or larger)
drawing paper or tagboard
glue, tape, or glue stick
colored markers and/or puffy paints
collage materials, such as:
    fabric trim, lace, magazine clippings, wallpaper scraps, wood curls, and wood scraps,
collected items, such as:
    bottle caps, corks, dried flowers, hair barrette, shells, small stones, and toothpicks
additional colored paper
scissors

Process

1. Cut out the central figure's shape or portrait from the fine art print. Glue it to drawing paper or tagboard. Let the glue dry.
2. Decorate and embellish the figure in some way both on and around the figure with drawing and collage materials. Changing the original figure creates a "parody" or changed likeness of the original. For example, add lace and fabric trims, beads and sequins to the figure's clothing.
3. Create a background scene or patterned background. Accent with pens and puffy paints, if desired.
4. Fashion a frame for the parody from another sheet of colored paper. Draw fancy designs on the frame to resemble ornately carved frames of long ago. Tape or glue the frame to the parody.

Internet Websites

- ArtSparx.com has excellent choices of human figures and faces offered by era, including a new section called "Art for Children." http://www.artsparx.com
- AllPosters.com offers a large selection of Renaissance prints as well as numerous other categories. http://www.allposters.com
- Browse 10,000 subjects, including children's favorites, and 7,000 artists at Art.com. http://www.art.com

2

Paint & Print

I don't paint things. I only paint the difference between things.

—Henri Matisse, artist (1869–1954)

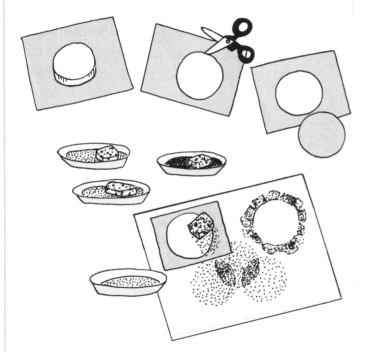

Sponge Dabbed Stencil

Create positive and negative stencil prints from a traced jar lid. Dab the stencils with sponges dipped in tempera paints.

Materials

tempera paints

one paper plate for each color of tempera paint

sponge cut into 2" to 3" (5cm to 7.5cm) squares or other shapes

jar lid

tagboard square

pencil

scissors

oil pastels

Process

1. Pour a puddle of tempera paint on a paper plate. Each plate will have a different color.
2. Moisten sponge squares with water and squeeze them dry. Place one sponge next to each plate of paint.
3. Place the lid of a jar in the center of a tagboard square leaving a good-sized 2" (5cm) border of tagboard around the jar lid. Trace the lid with a pencil.
4. To preserve both positive and negative stencils, slowly and carefully poke the point of a scissors through the tagboard on a point of the circle pencil line. Carefully cut out the circle. When finished, there will be a circle, which is a positive stencil, and the frame, which is a negative stencil.
5. Place one of the stencils on the paper. Lightly dab a sponge in the paint. Then dab paint around the outside edges of the positive stencil or the inside edges of the negative stencil. Make a pattern of paint using different colors and both stencils as desired. Let colors and stencil shapes overlap.
6. Then let the print dry.
7. For additional design interest, highlight and add details to the dry painting with oil pastels (Craypas™).

For Budding Artists

- Dab a damp sponge in paint and make sponge prints on paper.
- Spray a hand-misting spray bottle of water on plain paper, cardboard, or a chalkboard.

Spray Painting

Original stencil designs are arranged on white paper and misted over with watercolor paint.

Materials

choice of paint:
  food coloring mixed to a bright color
    with a little water
  Liquid Watercolors™
  tempera paint thinned with water
4-oz. spray bottles, one for each color
large sheet of white paper
scissors
pencil
tagboard
stencils (shapes cut from tagboard or heavy
  paper, both the outside negativepiece
  and the inside positive piece (see
  illustration)

flat (washable) objects or shapes, such as:
  hammer
  kitchen tools
  magnifying glass
  paper clips
  ruler
  scissors
  other ideas
choice of materials to sprinkle on wet
  paint:
  crushed chalk
  powdered tempera paint
  powdery glitter
  table salt

Process

1. Choose to mix food coloring to a bright color with water or mix tempera paint with water to thin.

2. Fill several small spray bottles with the paint, one bottle for each color.

3. Cut shapes from tagboard for stencils (see Sponge Dabbed Stencil on the previous page for trace-and-cut technique). Collect flat objects with interesting shapes. Objects should be washable if they will be used again.

Hint: Natural objects such as leaves and sticks are effective as stencils for a nature theme.

4. Place stencils or flat objects on a large sheet of white paper.

5. Spray a fine mist of paint over the stencil.

6. Next, reposition the stencil or objects to overlap painted areas. Spray again with a different color.

7. While paint is still very wet, sprinkle crushed chalk, powdered paint, table salt, or powdery glitter over the sprayed designs. If the painting is not wet, mist a little water over the areas selected. Tap off any extra sprinkled material onto newspaper.

8. Allow the painting to dry.

Shimmer Paint

Mix white glue with tempera paint to create art on aluminum foil. The resulting creation will shimmer and shine.

Materials

heavy-duty aluminum foil

cardboard

tape

tempera paints or food coloring

white glue

small container for each color of paint

paintbrushes, one for each color

Process

1. Wrap a sheet of heavy-duty aluminum foil around a square of cardboard, folding edges of foil around the cardboard to the back. Press out wrinkles and smooth as much as possible. Tape loose edges on the back of the cardboard.

2. Mix a little tempera paint or food coloring with white glue in a small container. Make as many colors as desired, each in a separate container. Stir with a paintbrush to mix each color.

3. Paint with the colored glue on the foil. It will look thick and milky at this stage.

4. Allow the painting to dry overnight or over a weekend until the painting is clear, shimmery, and shiny.

For Budding Artists

- Squeeze and bend aluminum foil.
- Paint on aluminum foil with tempera paints mixed with a little dish detergent.

Gloss Watercolor

What a great use for old watercolor paints! Mix softened watercolor paints with gloss polymer hobby coating to make a glossy, bright, and smooth paint.

Materials

old watercolor paint box

water

small paper cups

gloss polymer hobby coating (ModPodge™ is one excellent common brand
(non-toxic liquid sealer, glue, and finish for wood, paper, fabric, and other porous
surfaces that cleans up with soap and water)

soft paintbrush

drawing paper

permanent medium-point markers, one or many colors (or a heavy black permanent
marker)

Process

1. Fill an old, used watercolor box with a little water and let soften for about 5 minutes.
2. While waiting, fill a small paper cup with a teaspoon or so of ModPodge™ or other gloss medium.
3. Dip a soft paintbrush in the softened watercolor paint, and stir this into the cup of ModPodge™.
4. Paint with the watercolor-gloss mixture on drawing paper. Note how it goes on milky in appearance, but dries to a shiny bright gloss.
5. When the painting is dry, outline or add designs with permanent medium-point markers. Outlining with a heavy permanent black marker is very effective.

Lovely Leaf Resist

Crayon resist is an art technique in which the wax in the crayon resists the water in the paint. This easy-to-do crayon resist captures the natural beauty and design of leaves.

Materials

large supple leaves, varying sizes and shapes

drawing paper

pencil

crayons

watercolor paints

wide, soft paintbrush

jar of water

facial tissues for water puddles

Process

1. Trace leaves on drawing paper with a pencil. Use varying sizes and shapes of leaves, overlapping the outlines.

   Hint: Shapes of any kind—not just leaves—may be used in this activity.

2. Add details inside the leaf shapes with any colors of crayons such as veins, spots, and textures. Colors found in leaves in nature are not required. Choose colors to enjoy.

3. Trace over the outside lines of the leaves with black or other dark colored crayon.

4. To complete the resist, paint over the crayon leaf drawings with a wide, soft brush heavily dripping with watercolor paint. (Note how the wax crayon resists the watery paint, but the paint holds to the uncolored areas of paper.)

5. Coat the entire paper and all crayon lines with paint. Then let the painting dry. Extra paint puddles may be absorbed with facial tissues.

For Budding Artists

● Draw with crayon. Paint over the crayon with thinned tempera or watercolor paints.

Oil Pastel Resist

Draw with oil pastels and wash over the drawing with tempera paint—another experience with resist. The oil in the oil pastel resists the water in the paint.

Materials

heavy construction paper, black

oil pastels, such as Craypas™

make-up sponge or other small sponge

tempera paint thinned with water

container

water

wide, soft paintbrush

paper clip

gloss polymer and sponge brush (optional)

Process

1. Draw heavily on the black construction paper with oil pastels in bright, intense colors. Create any design or picture, blending and mixing the oil pastels with a makeup sponge.
2. Paint over the oil pastel drawing with a contrasting color of slightly thinned tempera paint. Bright blue, purple, black, or white are striking. The oil pastel will resist the tempera paint causing the pastels to show through the paint.
3. As an additional design idea, scratch designs and textures through the oil pastel art with a paper clip that has been straightened.
4. When the painting is dry, preserve it by brushing with gloss polymer and a sponge brush, if desired. Dry once again.

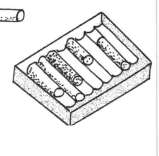

Tempera Paint

Easy Squeezy Batik

Paint with watercolors over a flour and water design; then break the flour away, to reveal a batik resist.

Materials

For flour paste:
- 1 cup water
- 1 cup flour
- 4 teaspoons alum (in the supermarket spice aisle)

measuring cups and spoons
electric mixer or blender
squeeze bottle (picnic ketchup type or empty shampoo)

square of white fabric, washed and dried, approximately 12" x 12" (30cm x 30cm)
old towel
masking tape
watercolor paints
paintbrush
dish of water
newspapers
cardboard square, approximately 10" x 10" (25cm x 25cm)

Process

1. With adult help, make the flour paste. Start with 1 cup water. Add 1 cup flour and 4 teaspoons alum. Mix with an electric mixer or blender until smooth. Pour the paste into a squeeze bottle.
2. Spread the fabric square on the old towel. Tape the towel to the table and the fabric to the towel with masking tape.
3. Squeeze a flour-paste design on the fabric using thick lines and fat dots. Leave undisturbed overnight to dry.
4. With very wet, bright watercolors, paint the areas between the paste lines. Painting over the paste lines is fine too. Dry several hours or overnight.
5. Remove the tape. Bend and crack the flour paste to remove. Rub, crumble, and break away all the paste lines. Work over the sink or newspapers. When all the paste has been removed, the batik fabric will reveal its brilliance.

Display Idea

- Turn the batik over and place the cardboard square in the center. Fold the edges of the batik around the cardboard and tape with masking tape to hold.

Fabric Ideas

- Create the easy batik on a T-shirt, apron, pillowcase, placemats or napkins. Always wash and dry the fabric before using so fabric will accept bright color.

For Budding Artists

- Mix 1 part flour, 1 part salt, and 1 part water. Pour into a squeeze bottle. Squeeze designs on paper or cardboard.
- Paint with water-based ink or thinned tempera paints on plain paper.

True Resist

India ink is the necessary ingredient in exploring a true wax resist. Dress in worry-free art clothes.

Materials

chalk

white or light-colored construction paper

tempera paints and brushes

art smock, waterproof apron, or art clothes

plastic sheeting or newspapers

India ink (office supply, art, or craft store)

soft brush

paper towels

gloss polymer hobby coating

sponge brush

Process

1. Draw a simple, bold picture or design with chalk on white or light-colored construction paper.

2. Paint around the chalk outlines with tempera paints. Let the paint reach just to the chalk outline, but don't cover it. Dry completely.

3. Cover the table with plastic or thick newspaper. Wear art clothes or other protective coverings. Place the drawing on the table covering. Generously brush the dry, tempera-painted surface with India ink. Let dry in place.

4. Still wearing art clothes, and with paper towels handy, rinse off dry India ink under the water faucet at the sink. Keep the water turned to a low pressure to begin. Ink may be brushed gently with fingers to encourage it to loosen from the chalk areas.

5. Place the painting on newspaper on a table or floor. Blot with paper towels to dry. Let dry for several hours. When the painting is completely dry, coat with gloss polymer using a sponge brush. Dry again.

Gel Comb Painting

Fingerpainting takes on a whole new look and feel when paint is mixed with hair gel and comb designs are pulled through the paint.

Materials

tempera paints

hair gel (inexpensive variety)

small container, one for each color paint

wide paintbrush

generic copier paper, white or colored (or use the backs of recycled paper instead)

old credit cards (any plastic cards) or combs with various widths of teeth

extra-fine glitter (optional)

heavy book or other heavy object (or warm iron and newsprint)

Process

1. Mix equal parts tempera paint and hair gel in a small container to a consistency of thick finger paint. With a wide paintbrush, cover the entire surface of the paper with the mixture.

2. Pre-cut edges of plastic cards in interesting comb designs (see illustrations) to make dragging tools. Pull or drag designs through the paint with the edges of the cards. Create straight lines, swirls, basket weaves, or any other design. Plastic combs with various widths of teeth can also be used. Feel free to incorporate fingerpainting techniques or other tools of interest.

3. As an optional step, sprinkle the painting with glitter while it is still wet.

4. Let the painting dry overnight. (When dry, flatten the painting by pressing it under a heavy book or other heavy object for a day or two. The painting can also be pressed carefully between sheets of newsprint with a warm iron set to heat without steam.)

5. Enjoy the painting as it is, or cut to make bookmarks, note cards, or endpapers for homemade books.

For Budding Artists

- Fingerpaint on plain large paper with tempera paints, mixing two or more colors.

- Paint with dark tempera paint over a crayon drawing.

RAD (Remarkably Active Design)

Paint designs with fingers, incorporating expressive movements and actions.

Materials

large drawing paper
watercolor paints
wide brushes
jar of water

black tempera paint
soapy water
fingernail brush
old towel

Process

1. Paint drawing paper with large areas of watercolor paints in different colors. Let the colors overlap and intersect to create light and dark areas. Then dry.

2. First, think of an action or descriptive word to incorporate in the painting. Moving the fingers and hands in this way will be reflected in the art. Some word choices are:

Action words	Descriptive words
dance	freezing
hop	friendly
skip	happy
slide	loopy
sneak	sleepy
stomp	slow
tiptoe	jumpy
zigzag	angry

Tiptoe with Fingers

3. Pour a puddle of black tempera paint directly on the painting. Use hands to spread and smooth the paint to cover the paper. Make fingerpaint shapes and lines on the watercolor background using the actual movement or action depicted by the word. For example, tiptoe fingers through the paint making dot-like tracks, or lazily draw fingers that are sleepy and slow through the paint. Note where the watercolor areas change and overlap. Try to use both thick and thin lines for added interest.

4. While the painting is drying, scrub hands and nails with soapy water and a nailbrush. Dry with an old towel.

Hint: If the painting curls when dry, an adult can flatten it by lightly pressing it between two sheets of newsprint with an iron set to warm without steam.

Tempera Paint
Black

Watercolor Spin

Squeeze Liquid Watercolors™ onto a paper plate in a salad spinner. Spin the spinner and see the brilliant, moving results!

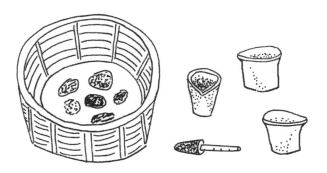

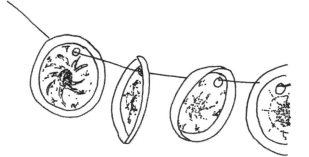

Materials

small paper cups
Liquid Watercolors™, 3 or 4 colors (may substitute food coloring gel paste diluted in
    water)
salad spinner
eyedropper
6" (10 cm) paper plates
thick newspaper drying area
yarn
hole punch (optional)

Process

1. Fill small paper cups ¼ full with Liquid Watercolors™. Pinch the rim of each cup to form a pouring spout. If using food coloring gel pastes, combine them with a little bit of water in small paper cups. Mix and stir with a stick or small paintbrush.
2. Place a small paper plate in the salad spinner. Slowly and carefully squeeze drops of color from an eyedropper or drizzle from a paintbrush directly on the plate. Secure the salad spinner lid. Spin!
3. Remove the lid and see the amazing effects of centrifugal force on paint! Add more paint to the same plate, or make a new design on a fresh plate. Create as many designs as desired, experimenting with colors and spinning force.
4. Cover a table or a section of the floor with a thick layer of newspapers. Let plates dry on the newspaper drying area.
5. Spin dry plates in the salad spinner to see how the design looks when it is moving.
6. Plates may be displayed by stringing yarn through a hole punched in each plate to make a long garland of colorful plates. The garland makes a festive, bright decoration for any celebration.

Hint: Use both sides of each plate.

For Budding Artists

• Paint with watercolor paints on plain paper. Tilt the paper to see the paint run this way and that.

Wavy Watercolors

Position a wavy stencil on paper and apply paint over its edge. Then reposition the stencils and paint again. Repeat several times.

Materials

old file folder

scissors

poster board or other heavy paper (any size from 8½" x 11" [20cm x 30cm] or larger)

watercolor paints or thin tempera paints, in colors from very light to very dark
   (examples: pastel yellow and green, bright purple and blue)

sponge brush or square of damp sponge

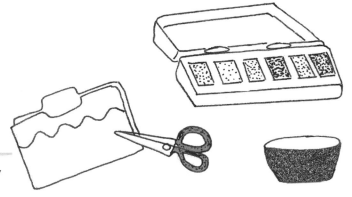

Process

1. Cut a rectangular shape, about 4" x 12" (10cm x 30cm) from a file folder. Cut a wavy line along one side of the rectangle (see illustration).

2. Position the wavy edge anywhere on the poster board. Beginning with the lightest color paint (perhaps yellow), dab or brush paint over the wavy edge onto the paper. Dry brush marks are fine, as are wetter paint areas. Dry briefly. Clean the brush or sponge between colors each time and dry the painting briefly before continuing.

3. Move the rectangle to a different position overlapping the first color. Select a second color that is slightly darker than the first (perhaps light green). With a clean sponge brush or sponge square, repeat painting over the edge onto the paper once again. Dry briefly.

4. Move the wavy stencil again, and repeat the technique using the next darker color. Continue repeating the repositioning of the stencil until the poster board looks like waves of colors layered on one another. Then dry the finished artwork completely.

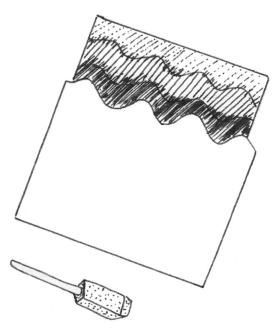

Hint: Lines within the design may be highlighted, if preferred, with any choice of coloring tools, including: crayons, oil pastels, colored markers, pencils, or metallic markers.

Torn Watercolor Illusion

Thick, dampened paper is painted with blurry watercolor paints. When torn into strips and mounted in place, the irregular edges of the work will add to the artistic design.

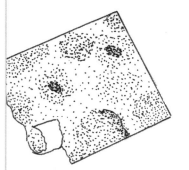

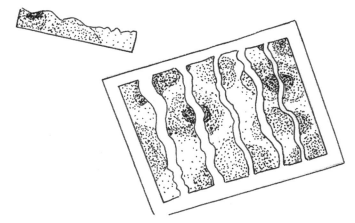

Materials

watercolor paper or other absorbent thick paper (desk blotter or pressed fiber paper)
sponge brush
watercolor paints, any variety
paintbrush
jar of water
second sheet of paper for background
glue

Process

1. Dampen absorbent or thick paper with water using a sponge brush. The paper should be wet but not soaked. Brush a little water on the table, too. Smooth the paper onto the damp table so the paper will stick.
2. Paint with watercolor paints on the wet paper, allowing the colors to blend and blur. Create designs and areas that mix and blend. When the paper is filled with color, allow it to dry briefly on the table.

Hint: Try splattering dots of paint here and there.

3. While still damp, carefully tear the paper into four or five strips. Work slowly, making little tears bit by bit. The edges should be irregular and rough in texture.
4. Position the strips in order on a background paper with space left between.
5. Spread glue on the back of a strip. Glue the strip down, maintaining spaces between strips. Do this for all of the strips. Then let dry.

For Budding Artists

- Paint on thick paper with watercolor paints. Tear the painting into strips or squares. Glue it back together on a background paper.

Seeing Double

Seeing double is only half the fun! Create a pleated accordion-style artwork where a painted image is folded accordion style into alternating colorful and negative strips.

Materials

pencil
large, white drawing paper
tempera paints, paintbrushes
jar of water for rinsing

black tempera paint and brush,
 or black marker
strip of cardboard and tape

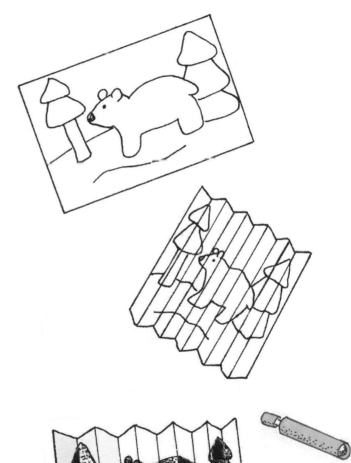

Process

1. Draw a simple bold design or picture with pencil that fills the entire space of the drawing paper. Try to draw something that covers the paper from left edge to right edge, and from top to bottom.

2. Next, fold the drawing accordion style (like a paper fan) into sections no smaller than 1" (2cm) each, and no larger than 3" (7cm). Fold back and forth until the paper is completely folded. Press the edges to make sharp folds. Then flatten the paper on the table.

3. **Painting Step 1**: Paint the drawing on every other section only. That is, paint the first section, but skip the second, paint the third, but skip the fourth, and so on. Painting every other section is an alternating pattern. Dry about one hour or more, until smudging is minimal. **Painting Step 2**: Choose to paint with black, or to use a black marker. Both techniques work equally well. On the sections that are unpainted, use only black to finish the painting. These sections will be black and white when complete. Then let dry completely, at least one hour.

4. Refold the accordion pleats. Tape a strip of cardboard all the way across the back of the accordion to help keep the accordion folds in place. There will be alternating stripes of colorful and negative on the same painting. The painting should stand up easily for display.

5. Look at the painting from different angles to appreciate the visual contrast of positive and negative alternating design.

Scribble Dribble

Drizzle colored glue from high above a large sheet of paper to create shiny, glossy works of art guaranteed to be artists' favorites.

Materials

food coloring

white glue

cups for colored glue

thick paintbrushes, spoons, or wooden craft sticks

large paper

Process

1. Mix food coloring with glue, each color in a separate cup.
2. Place the paper on the floor. Kneel on a chair next to the table and the paper.
3. Dip a brush, spoon, or stick into the thick, drippy colored glue.
4. Holding it high above the paper, gently wiggle, swirl, and move the brush to drip lines, drizzles, dots, dribbles, and shapes of colored glue on the paper.
5. Repeat this action with more than one color.
6. When dry, the artwork will be glossy, shiny, and colorful.

For Budding Artists

- Drizzle paint from a brush or spoon onto paper.
- Draw with drizzled or dripped white glue. Sprinkle with glitter.

Glue Line Design

Drawing with white glue squeezed from the bottle imparts a bold outline calling for embellishment with watercolor paint and art tissue.

Materials

white glue

black ink (or black paint)

squeeze bottles

pencil or ballpoint pen

white drawing paper

watercolor paints

paintbrush

colored tissue paper

liquid starch or thinned white glue

Process

1. With adult help, mix black ink (or black paint) with white glue. Pour into squeeze bottle.
2. Make a drawing with pencil or ballpoint pen on white drawing paper.
3. Trace over the larger lines and major shapes with black glue. Let dry completely, usually overnight.
4. Paint with watercolors inside the black outlined areas of the drawing.
5. Arrange pieces of colored art tissue on the rest of the drawing's background. Brush tissue with thinned white glue or liquid starch to adhere. Allow to dry.

Clay Paint

Press bits of clay onto poster board, creating a thick impressionistic painting that invites experimentation with color mixing.

Materials

assorted colors of plasticine modeling clay or bright playdough

heavy paper plate

masking tape (optional)

poster board, any color

Process

1. Make a clay palette. Select an assortment of plasticine modeling clay or playdough colors, and place blobs on a heavy paper plate.
2. Secure the palette to the worktable with masking tape, if desired.
3. Pinch a bit of clay from the palette and smear or press it onto the poster board. Continue adding clay to the poster board, creating a thick "painting."

Hint: Clay colors can be blended together directly on the palette to make mixed and swirled colors, or they can be mixed as the painting is created directly on the poster board.

For Budding Artists

- Model with playdough and play clay.
- Fingerpaint with two or more colors on plain paper.

Swirly Whirls

Squeeze paint onto paper plates and swirl with a fork to create an intriguing marbled effect.

Materials

small squeeze bottles, one for each paint color
   (may substitute small brushes or eyedroppers)
tempera paints, several colors
6" (10cm) paper plates
fork
toothpick
scissors
paper punch

Process

1. Fill small squeeze bottles each with a different color of tempera paint. Squeeze squiggly lines of paint on a small paper plate. (Or drip paint from small brushes or eyedroppers instead of squeeze bottles.) Choose two colors minimum, or as many as eight.

2. To add more color and design at this stage, shave chalk dust on the wet paint. It will float and add to the color in the marbling and swirling.

3. Tilt the plate in all directions and watch the paint move and mix. To encourage the marbling, lightly drag a fork through the paint.

Hint: To make "chains of hearts," place dots of color in a line or ring and drag a toothpick through.

4. Make as many marbled plates as desired, experimenting with different marbling effects and mixing of colors.

5. Allow all the plates to dry completely. Then turn the plates over and repeat marbling the opposite sides of all the plates. Dry again.

Hint: The opposite side of the plate can also be designed with crayon, markers, or collage instead of paint.

6. Punch a hole in each plate and thread with string or yarn. Create a garland of continuous plates (knot yarn between each plate), or hang plates individually from a pushpin in the ceiling or above a window. The plates will move in the air currents, showing both sides of the design.

Crystal Winter

Draw a winter scene with crayon on white paper. Then wash over the drawing with watery blue tempera. For the final touch, sprinkle with salt to form snowy crystals in the paint.

Materials

crayons, including blue and white

heavy white paper or watercolor paper

watercolor or tempera paint, blue

water

wide soft paintbrush

salt in a shaker

Process

1. With a light blue crayon on heavy white paper or watercolor paper, draw a snowy outdoor scene. (A country scene might include trees, fence, snowman, stream, and a pond. A city scene might include tall buildings, brick wall, iron fence, trees, lamppost, and a street sign.)

   Hint: If a more free-form abstract crystal painting is preferred, draw swirly lines and shapes instead of a scene.

2. Color heavily with white crayon for the ground (snow). Leave the sky uncolored or blank.

3. With thinned blue tempera paint or blue watercolor paint, wash over the entire paper. While the paint is still wet, sprinkle the painting with salt. The salt will dissolve in the paint and create a snowy crystal result.

Theme Idea

- Instead of a winter theme, use other colors and designs. The salt will still do its crystal magic, but will not relate to winter or ice.

For Budding Artists

- Draw with crayon on plain paper. Paint over the crayon with watercolor paint.
- Paint with watercolor paint on plain paper. Sprinkle with salt when finished.

Sparkly Layered Snow

Paint with a solution of Epsom salts over oil pastel snowflake designs to create a swirling sparkly work of art.

Materials

Epsom salts

water

sauce pan and stovetop or heat plate

jar with lid

large drawing paper, 18" x 24" (45cm x 60cm)

oil pastels

wide soft brush

white tissue paper

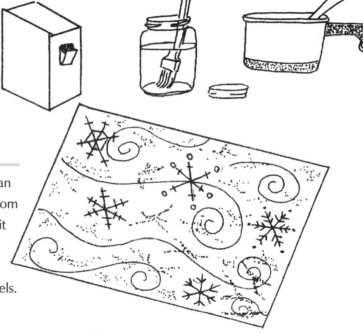

Process

1. Make the Salt Solution (adult-only): Fill a jar with water. Pour into a saucepan. Add an equal amount of Epsom salts to the water. (For example: 1 cup water and 1 cup Epsom salts, or 3 cups water and 3 cups Epsom salts.) Heat on the stove, stirring the salt as it dissolves. Some salt may not dissolve, which is to be expected. Let cool. Pour the solution into a jar. Keep the lid handy to store unused solution.

2. On a large sheet of drawing paper, draw long flowing and swirling lines with oil pastels. A variety of colors may be used, or white only is also effective.

3. Add drawings of snowflakes with three intersecting lines (to make six points). More lines can be added to the basic snowflake shapes to make each one unique.

4. Paint over the drawing with the Epsom salts and water solution. Press white tissue paper over all. Dry completely. The tissue will take on a sparkly appearance.

5. Lightly draw more snowflakes or swirling lines on the dry tissue with a pencil, if desired.

Theme Idea

- Instead of a snow subject, create with other colors and designs. The salt mixture will still do its crystal magic, but will not relate to snow.

Double Dip Shading

Shape playdough into a chunky, hand-sized form to dip into double colors of paint, creating shaded prints all in one step.

Materials

playdough (or any play clay or
   modeling clay)
two colors of tempera paint, light
   and dark
additional colors of tempera paint
   (optional)
paintbrush
flat tray or plate
practice paper

choice of large paper, such as:
   colorful art tissue
   construction paper
   craft paper, on roll
   newspaper classified pages
   newsprint
   plain wrapping paper
   poster board
   reverse side of old poster
   tissue paper
   white wrapping paper

Process

1. Form a big handful of playdough into a simple geometric or abstract shape, or into the shape of a familiar object. Pat the shape gently on the table to make one side of the dough flat for the printing in the next step.
2. Pour one puddle each of two colors of tempera paint side by side on a flat tray or plate. Dip half of the playdough shape into one color, and the other half into the other color. Press the playdough on the practice paper to make a print. Notice how the colors mix and cause a two-tone shaded image. Practice a few more times to get a mixture of colors that works nicely. Add two more paint colors to a second tray if more colors are needed. Additional playdough shapes may also be formed. Make a few more practice prints before beginning the actual artwork.
3. Make shaded prints on the large paper. Create any pattern for covering the paper. When the paper is dry, use for wrapping paper or enjoy and display as art.

For Budding Artists

- Make prints by dipping objects in paint and pressing on paper.
- Draw a shape, paint it, and cut the shape out.

Shadow Shapes

Trace objects to make shapes on white paper, and paint them. Cut out the shapes and pair with an identical shape. One shape becomes a shadow of the other.

Materials

objects to trace to make shapes, such as:

    cassette tape case
    CD jewel case
    jar lid
    small box

white paper
gray or black construction paper
tempera paints
paintbrush
scissors
glue stick
colored construction paper

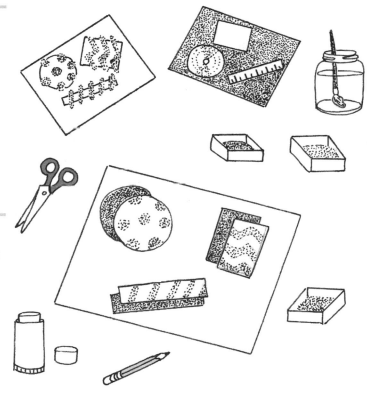

Process

1. Select one or two objects to trace. Objects that make squares, circles, rectangles, and triangles work best. Trace a shape on the white paper, and make an identical shape on the dark paper. Trace more shapes on both papers, always making a matching pair.

2. Paint the white paper shapes with tempera paints. Choose to paint solid colors or patterns and designs. Painting slightly over the lines will not be a problem. Let the paintings dry. Meanwhile, cut out the dark shapes. Then cut out the dry painted shapes.

3. Pair up a painted shape with a dark shape. Position a dark shape on the background paper, and glue in place. Then glue the identical painted shape over it, but off center slightly (see illustration). The dark shape will look like a shadow of the painted shape.

4. Fill the background paper with a pattern of painted shapes with their shadows behind them.

Natural Painting

Rub paper with grasses, flower blossoms, sticks, bark bits, and other collected nature items to create a naturally mixed drawing and painting.

Materials

white paper
glue (optional)
several sheets of drawing paper
assorted collected nature items, such as:

    bark chunks (garden bark)
    berries
    dandelions
    flower blossoms
    fresh leaves
    grasses
    lump of hard soil
    mud
    twigs & sticks
    weeds

Process

1. Experiment with making marks on the first sheet of paper. Explore rubbing leaves, grasses, blossoms, and other natural bits of nature to see which materials are best for color, shading, or outline. Try some thin, light and dark, bold markings.
2. When comfortable with the natural materials and their effects, create a planned artwork. Think of a design or picture to create with the natural materials. For example, draw a vase with bark marks, draw flower stems with green grasses pressed onto the paper, and blossoms with smeared dandelion blossoms.
3. For additional interest, glue leaves, blossoms, and other natural materials onto artwork.

For Budding Artists

● Draw and color with twigs or bark on white paper, like using a crayon or pencil. Scratch designs capturing the natural color of the twigs or bark.

Floral Imprint on Fabric

Pounding and crushing as arrangement of fresh leaves or blossoms creates a naturally beautiful print on fabric.

Materials

square of muslin or other cotton fabric, approximately 12″ x 12″ (30cm x 30cm)
    (an old white T-shirt cut to size works well)
pad of newspaper on a work table
assortment of fresh leaves, weed blossoms, stems, and flowers
sheet of white paper bigger than the fabric square
tape
rubber mallet or wooden block

Process

1. Place the fabric on a pad of newspaper. Arrange a design with the leaves, flowers, and other natural plant materials on the fabric. Allow them to overlap in places. Place a bigger sheet of white paper over the design and tape it down.

2. With adult help and supervision, use a rubber mallet or wooden block to hammer on the white paper, covering the entire surface of the paper, crushing the flowers and leaves underneath. Tap and hammer over the entire paper once again, releasing the natural colors and juices of the plants into the fabric and paper.

Hint: Hammering with moderate pressure works best. Go easy so paper does not tear.

3. Carefully remove the tape and lift the paper. Brush and pick the crushed items from the fabric. Light pastel designs will have transferred to both the fabric and the paper in matching patterns.

Display Idea

- Tape both artworks—fabric and paper—behind individual framing mattes, and display on the wall as a pair.

Precious Jewel Case

Paint a design on the inside of a CD or audio cassette jewel case. When the case is closed, the painted design will be smooth and glossy in a self-framed display box.

Materials

clear plastic jewel case (box that holds a CD and/or audio cassette), clean and dry
acrylic paints or Liquitex Glossies™, specifically made for painting on glossy surfaces
small paintbrush
water
wet sponge for wiping fingers

Process

1. Open the plastic jewel case. On the inside surface, paint a picture, design, words, or any other ideas with acrylic paints. Paints may be thinned with water to make them spread smoothly.

Hint: Paint words or letters reversed. Peek at the outside of the jewel case every now and then to see how the design is going.

2. When the painting is done, leave the jewel case open to dry.
3. To display, stand the jewel case with its sides angled slightly open with the paintings facing out. A jewel case will also stand up when closed.

Photograph Idea

- Tape or glue a photograph in the jewel case with room around the edges. Paint a frame or designs around the picture on the open area. The case will be a natural framed display.

For Budding Artists

- Draw with colored markers on a scrap of wood.
- Draws with colored markers on plastic, Plexiglas, a window, or a mirror. Wipe clean.

Oh, Gouache!

Paint a design with gouache—a solid watercolor paint—on white-washed wood.

Materials

block of wood

sandpaper, medium grade

permanent black or brown marker (black for a bold look, brown for a natural look)

gouache paints (may substitute tempera paints), white required
   (gouache is available from any art or craft store)

plastic lids or other small containers for paint, one for each color of paint

water

paintbrushes

spray finish such as hair spray or clear acrylic paint (optional)

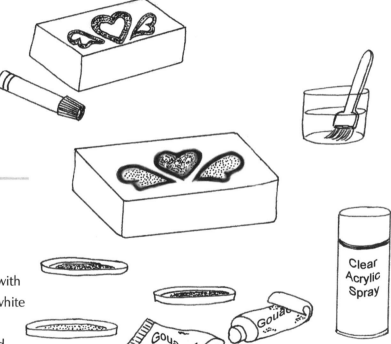

Process

1. Choose a block of scrap wood. Sand the edges of the block with medium-grade sandpaper to smooth rough edges.
2. Draw a design on the block with a dark brown (or black) permanent marker.
3. Squeeze a 1″ (5 cm) puddle of white gouache on a plastic lid. Add water with a paintbrush to make a thin wash of the white. Paint over the entire block of wood with thinned white color. Avoid painting directly on the brown or black lines. Painting white inside the spaces is fine. Then let dry briefly.
4. Select several more colors of gouache. Squeeze a little of each color on a plastic lid. Use it thick, or thin it slightly with water.
5. Fill in the design with colors over the white wash, leaving some areas white. Avoid painting directly over the pen lines.
6. Retrace any faded pen lines when the paint is dry again, if needed. An adult can spray the artwork with a fixative to add shine and bring out color.

Rock & Roll!

Plunk a rock into a coffee can and shake it up with multiple colors of paint.

Materials

tempera paints, several colors
small cups
small paper plate
coffee can with lid
small rocks and flat stones, clean and dry
plastic spoons
newspaper
fingernail polish, clear

Process

1. Pour tempera paints into small cups, one for each color.
2. Place a small paper plate inside a coffee can. Push the plate all the way in to the bottom, letting the sides of the plate cave in some, if necessary.
3. Choose a rock and use a plastic spoon to dip it in paint. Then drop the paint-covered rock in the coffee can. Dip more rocks in other colors of paint, and toss them in the can together.
4. Snap on the lid, and shake the can with both hands (hold the lid at the same time so it doesn't come loose). Shake and shake until the rocks are well covered in paint.
5. Pour the rocks out on newspaper. Look at all the mixed swirling colors and designs.
6. Let the rocks dry completely. When dry, paint with clear fingernail polish to add shine.

For Budding Artists

- Paint smooth stones or rocks with plain water.
- Draw on rocks with crayon.
- Roll a marble through paint in a round cake pan with a paper lining.
- Draw with colored markers on ceramic tile.

Ceramic Tile Painting

With liquid acrylic paint, decorate ceramic tiles and then bake in the oven for a permanent result.

Materials

glazed tile square

soap and water

pencil

liquid acrylic paints, such as:

    Liquitex Acrylic Glossies™

plastic lid or palette (optional)

small paintbrush

water

cup

rag or towel

cookie sheet with edges

oven

4 stick-on felt circles

Process

1. Wash the tile with soap and water to remove grease and dust. Dry well.

2. Draw a design on the tile with a pencil. Marks will not erase, but can be washed away with soap and water.

3. Open the paint jars. If mixing colors, do so on a plastic lid or palette.

Hint: Use only a little bit of paint to start, as it dries within an hour and cannot be reused. Water-based acrylic paints can be thinned with water. Use them to paint on glass, wood, ceramic tiles, plastic, metal, and other glossy surfaces. They are non-toxic and dry glossy.

4. Paint directly on the tile with a small brush. Paint may overlap or layer. When the painting is complete, wash the brush in soap and water.

5. To heat-set the paint, with adult help, place the tile on a cookie sheet in the center of a cool oven. Heat the oven to 325°F [162°C]. Then set the timer for 30 minutes. The tile will bake to a hard ceramic finish in 30–40 minutes. Then turn off the oven. Let the tile cool down in the oven with the door closed for an hour or more.

6. When cool, press sticky-felt circles on the back of the tile, one on each of the four corners. This will protect the table surface and allow the tile to be used as a trivet.

Marker Monoprint

A single image is printed from a colored-marker drawing pressed onto wet paper.

Materials

paper (copier paper, drawing paper, or any variety)
colored markers, water-based (not permanent)
Styrofoam grocery tray, clean and dry
old towels
sponge
water

Process

1. Turn over a Styrofoam grocery tray (the ordinary white variety used for packaging vegetables, meats, or sushi). Draw a picture on the flat smooth back of the tray. Go over the drawing heavily with a colored marker so the lines are wet with color.
2. Place a sheet of paper on a pad of old towels. Moisten the paper with a water-filled sponge, smoothing the paper on the towel.
3. Turn over the drawing and place it on the moist paper. Press the grocery tray straight onto the paper firmly, without wiggling it around. Carefully lift the tray from the paper.
4. The resulting print will be a blurred reverse of the original drawing.
5. More color can then be added to the print, if preferred.

For Budding Artists

- Draw with colored markers on plain paper. Paint on marker lines with water.
- Press a thumb to an inkpad, and make thumbprints on plain paper.

Mingled Mono-Draw

Roll water-based ink on a cookie sheet. Draw on paper placed over the ink. Is this a painting, a drawing, or a print? It's all three!

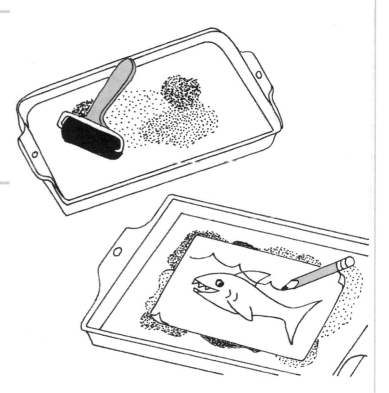

Materials

water-based printing ink, two or more colors
brayer or other roller
cookie sheet
white paper
pencil
wet sponge

Process

1. Squeeze a tablespoon or so of each tube of colored printing ink on the cookie sheet. Roll the blobs into a thin layer with the brayer or roller, letting the colors mix and overlap a bit. Cover an area of the cookie sheet with ink about the same size as the white paper by rolling the brayer back and forth.
2. Gently slip a piece of white paper onto the inked area. Do not press down.
3. Draw with a pencil on the white paper. Press down hard with the point of the pencil when drawing. Peek under the corner of the paper. There will be an ink print of the pencil drawing on the other side of the paper.
4. Reuse the same ink for more prints by rolling over it again with the brayer or roller. Add more ink, if needed.

Hint: Tempera paints or food coloring gel paste may be used, but printing ink works best.

Warm Press Print

Create a print lifted from a crayon design melted on a warming tray.

Materials

electric warming tray (thrift store, yard sale)
old crayons, peeled
white copier paper
paper towels

choice of protection for hands:
    kitchen hot mitt
    mittens
    small towel
    work gloves

Process

1. An adult should set up the warming tray on a table safely away from where others could bump into it. The cord should be directed to the back of the table, out of the way of others. Only one artist should work at a time, and an adult should be present to supervise for safety at all times.
2. Set the tray's heat to the lowest setting, "warm" or "low." Wear protection on hands, especially on the non-drawing hand, which is used to steady the artwork.
3. With peeled crayon stubs, draw directly on the warming tray's warm, smooth, and shiny surface. Draw slowly, letting the crayons melt and puddle to make a liquid picture. Always be cautious of the heat.
4. To lift a print, place a piece of ordinary white copier paper over the drawing. Gently pat and rub the paper with a gloved hand to help the crayon soak into the paper. Lift the paper by the corner to see the image. It will begin to dry quickly. Hold the paper up to the light. The warm melted wax from the crayons will soak into the paper and make it translucent.

Hint: Prints can be taped in a sunny window.

5. To clean the tray, wipe with paper towels. The warm crayon will come right off, but not completely from all edges and crevices. Use the warming tray for art only.

Idea

- Cover the tray with aluminum foil. Draw directly on the foil. Press paper on the foil and lift a print. The foil will hold a second design: peel from the warming tray and cool.

For Budding Artists

- Draw with crayons on paper that has been taped to the surface of an electric warming tray.
- Fingerpaint on paper using tempera paint mixed with liquid starch.

Monoprint Madness

Experiment with monoprints created from fingerpainted designs with other added techniques.

Materials

tempera paint (one or more colors)
cookie sheet
liquid starch
choices of paper (colored paper, patterned gift paper, white paper)
wet sponge
newspaper drying area (beside table)

design tools, such as:
   ball of aluminum foil (blot or press in paint)
   comb (drag through paint)
   large paper clip (swirl through paint)
   old credit card (twist, drag, or swipe through paint)
   pencil, point missing (draw in paint)
   small block (slide, pull, drag, or twist in paint)
   small sponge brush (drag through paint)
   small sponge piece (dab in paint)

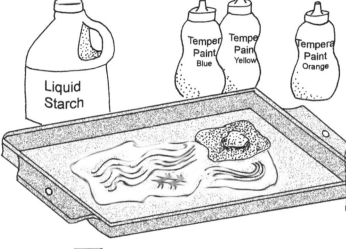
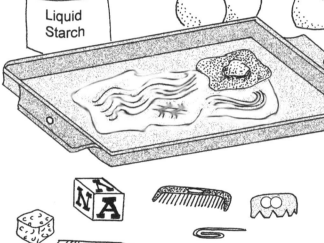

Process

1. Pour a small puddle of tempera paint on the cookie sheet. Add other colors in separate puddles if multi-colored prints are preferred. Pour a small puddle of liquid starch in the center of each paint puddle. Then mix and spread with bare hands.

   Hint: More starch than paint gives a thin translucent look. More paint than starch gives a heavier color look.

2. Make designs and drawings in the paint with fingers, fingernails, palms, or knuckles. Explore using other items and objects, like a comb, credit card, or ball of aluminum foil. Drag or press designs into the paint on the cookie sheet. When ready to make a print, wipe hands first with a wet sponge. Then gently slip a sheet of paper onto the design, and pat gently over the entire paper to capture the design and color. Lift and peel from the corner to see the captured print. Dry on newspaper.

3. Adjust colors and choose favorite design-making tools to create more specific prints and designs. Let all the prints dry on newspaper.

4. When dry, choose favorite prints to keep. The rest are experiments and can head to the recycle box or be cut into strips or squares for mosaic and collage projects.

Yarn Print

Glue yarn in any design on a paper plate. Roll ink over yarn, and lift a yarn collograph (collage and graphics combined) on paper.

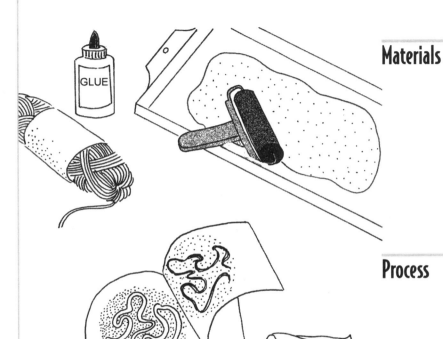

Materials

paper plate

yarn

glue

water soluble printing ink (craft or art supply store)

brayer or roller (small rolling pin, paint roller with handle)

cookie sheet

sheets of paper (white copier paper is perfect)

watercolor paints and brush, or markers (optional)

Process

1. Glue yarn to a paper plate in any design. Dry for several days or over a weekend.

2. Squeeze a blob of water-soluble ink on a cookie sheet. (Tempera paint may be used as a substitute.) Roll a brayer back and forth over the sheet to spread and smooth the ink and cover the brayer. Roll the inked brayer over the yarn. Roll in more ink and add extra ink to the yarn if needed.

3. Press a sheet of paper to the inky yarn, pat with the palms of the hands. To pick up a print, peel the paper from the design from the corner. Make as many prints from each inking as possible. Then re-ink, and make more prints!

4. When prints are dry, highlight with watercolor paints or colored markers.

For Budding Artists

- Press a variety of objects and junk into a puddle of paint to make prints on paper.
- Squeeze a glue design from the bottle on a paper plate.

Glue Line Relief Print

Dried glue designs become a raised relief perfect for creating remarkable prints.

Materials

cardboard or gift box lid

chalk or pencil

white glue in a squeeze bottle

printing ink (water soluble)

small brayer or roller

metal cookie sheet

choice of paper:

    newsprint

    newspaper classified pages

    white tissue paper

colored construction paper

tape

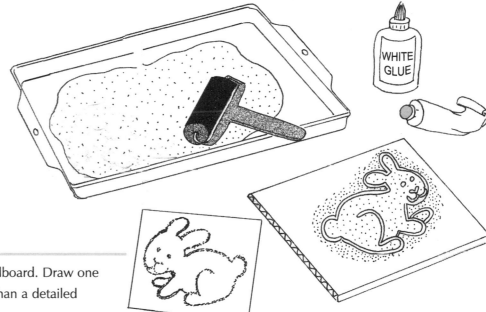

Process

1. Draw a bold and simple drawing with chalk or pencil on the cardboard. Draw one large subject, such as a single shape, like a fish or flower, rather than a detailed drawing.

2. Trace over the lines with white glue squeezed from the bottle. Dots and squiggles are good designs to add. Dry thoroughly overnight or a weekend.

3. Roll water-soluble ink with a brayer on a cookie sheet, spreading it smoothly. Then roll the inked brayer over the dry glue design.

4. To make a print, place newsprint or tissue on the inked design. Press with the palm of the hand from the center out to the edges. Capturing some of the inky background also looks good. Peel the paper from the ink to view the print. Make as many prints as desired.

5. Trim borders of favorite prints, and mount on colored construction paper.

Foil Collograph

A collograph combines collage (collo, or gluing things) with graphics (graph, or making prints). Make a paper scrap collage and cover it with foil. Use the collage to capture numerous ink prints.

Materials

paper scraps, thick and heavy
cardboard
scissors
glue
aluminum foil, heavy-duty
tape
blunt wooden pencil, cuticle stick,
   or craft stick

black ink or black tempera paint
   (any color is fine, black is
   strongest)
brush or sponge
any paper, one sheet for each print
paper towels

Process

1. Glue thick, heavy paper scraps to a cardboard background. The scraps can be cut into specific shapes, or used in their abstract scrap form.
2. Outline the shapes thickly with white glue squeezed from a glue bottle. Let the collage dry until the glue is no longer soft, usually about two days.
3. Cover the collage with a wide sheet of heavy-duty aluminum foil large enough to cover the entire surface. Leave at least one inch of extra foil on all sides to fold over the edges of the cardboard. Tape the foil edges on the back of the cardboard.
4. With a craft stick or a dull wooden pencil, gently and carefully press the foil down along the edges of the paper shapes and glue lines. Press in additional designs and details, if desired.
5. To make the collograph prints, spread black ink over the foil with a brush or sponge. Then press and pat a sheet of paper on the ink. Peel the paper away and lift a print. Set the print aside on newspaper to dry. Make several prints on additional sheets of paper. When the relief no longer gives a good print, re-ink and make more prints!
6. When finished, wipe the relief with paper towels to burnish the foil. (This means the ink will remain in the crevices and dents, but will wipe away from the raised and smooth surfaces. Some artists call this look "antique.") The foil becomes another artwork!

For Budding Artists

- Make a collage with a variety of materials glued on a paper plate.

Bright Tissue Collograph

Collage and graphics are combined in this bright and cheerful collage whose printing plate is equally artistic.

Materials

matte board square (matte squares and scraps with color or texture can be found free at framing shops)

white glue

gloss polymer medium and application brush

small brayer (or art roller, small rolling pin, or hard paint roller with handle)

water-soluble printing ink (craft store, office supply store)

cookie sheet

tissue paper, white or other colors

choices of textured collage materials, such as:

    Band-Aids

    bunion and corn pads

    confetti

    fabric

    gummed circles

    paper punches

    shoe insoles to cut into shapes

    stickers

    wallpaper

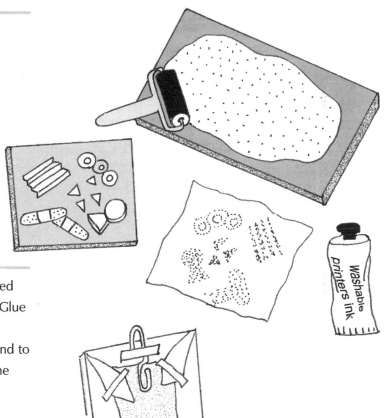

Process

1. Arrange an imaginative pattern on the background matte board square with textured collage materials. Shapes may overlap, but the collage should not to be too thick. Glue in place. Dry briefly.

2. With adult help, coat the collage with polymer gloss medium to seal the collage, and to keep shapes from coming off. Allow the gloss to dry until it is no longer sticky to the touch, usually overnight.

3. Squeeze some ink on a flat cookie sheet (no sides works best or the back of any baking sheet). Spread the ink smoothly with a brayer or other roller. Then roll ink on the collage.

4. Press a sheet of white wrapping tissue or colored art tissue to the inked collage. Press with the heel of the hand from the center out. Then peel and lift the print. Make as many prints as desired, re-inking as necessary.

Hint: Don't let ink dry, or the paper might stick to the ink.

5. Gently wipe excess ink from the collage with paper towels. Some ink will remain and adds to the artistic appearance. The collage is also an artwork!

6. Both the prints and the collage can be mounted for display.

Preparing the Prints for Displaying

To iron wrinkles from a tissue print, place between clean sheets of newsprint. Set the iron on warm and no steam (adult only). Display prints by wrapping around cardboard squares and taping the extra tissue on the back, or frame with used matte board.

Painted Transfer

Create an iron-on transfer for a T-shirt. Color the transfer with fabric paint.

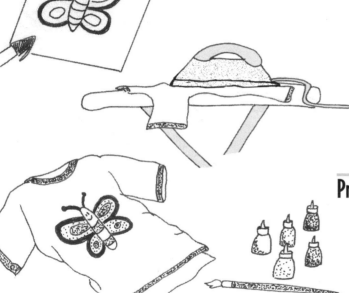

Materials

black pen
white paper
copy shop (such as Kinko's or U-Print)
T-shirt, or other fabric (pillowcase, apron, placemat, tablecloth, plain fabric)
paper or old towel
tape
fabric paint
paintbrushes

Process

1. Draw a simple black line drawing on paper with few details, much like a coloring book page.
2. Take the drawing and a plain white T-shirt to a copy shop or office store with copying services. Ask them to copy the drawing to a transfer sheet. Then they can heat-transfer the image to a T-shirt or other plain fabric.
3. After the image is transferred to the T-shirt, take the T-shirt home or to school and prepare to paint. Place paper or an old towel inside the T-shirt. Smooth the T-shirt out on a work table. Tape it in place.
4. Paint the spaces within the black line transfer with fabric paints and a small brush. Then dry. The shirt will wash-and-wear with bright colors through many washings and dryings.

For Budding Artists

- Draw with crayon on a plain T-shirt. Cover the T-shirt with an old towel and press the crayon into the fabric with an iron set on warm.
- Paint on fabric with watercolor paints.

Canvas Paint

Paint on a plain canvas fabric square. Pull a thread fringe and mount on a black background to highlight the colors and textures of painted canvas.

Materials

canvas fabric 12″ x 12″ (30cm x 30cm)

square of cardboard slightly larger than canvas

pencil

black permanent marker

watercolor paints

water

paintbrushes

black paper or black fabric to cover cardboard (slightly larger than cardboard)

masking tape or duct tape

fabric glue or tacky glue

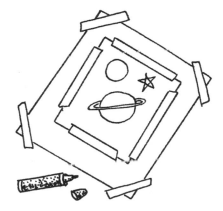

Process

1. Tape a 12″ [30cm] square of plain canvas fabric to cardboard (slightly larger than the fabric). Tape the cardboard to the table to add stability while working.
2. Draw a simple drawing or design with pencil on the canvas fabric.
3. Outline the design with black permanent marker.
4. Paint in and further outline the design with watercolor washes in any variety of colors.
5. When the fabric is dry, remove tape and cardboard.
6. Cover the cardboard with black paper or black fabric. Secure on the back with masking tape or duct tape.
7. Pull threads from all edges of the painted canvas to make fringe. Glue the painted canvas to the black background using fabric glue or tacky glue.

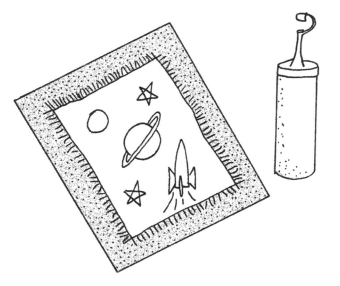

Cooperative Mural

Attach large paper to the wall. Two or more artists work together to plan and create a sizeable one-of-a-kind artwork.

Materials

large paper (craft paper from roll, other paper taped together)
masking tape or staples
pencils
drawing paper
tempera paints, variety of colors

plastic containers
paintbrushes
buckets of water
newspapers, old shower curtain, tarp, or old sheets

Process

1. Hang the paper securely on the wall by taping, tacking, or stapling.
2. Spread newspapers or other floor covering at the base of the wall to catch drips. Set out the paints, brushes and rinsing buckets for easy access.
3. The pair (or group) of artists will plan a theme and design for their cooperative painting. (Drawing a smaller version on a sheet of paper works well, but is not required.) Artists may also wish to decide on who paints which parts, or what techniques and steps to completion will be used.
   Some examples of large cooperative art:
   - art with a purpose (theme, message, or statement)
   - art that is abstract and visually exciting
   - art with humor or satire
   - art with multi-mixed techniques such as sponge painting and collage
4. Sketch the planned design or outlines of the artwork on the large paper.
5. Then begin painting! Letting painted areas dry between touching sections improves quality, but adds several days to complete the project.

Working With the Mural
- **Mattress Box Mural:** Instead of large paper, draw designs with chalk on a large mattress box. Fill in the exteriors of the designs with paint up to the chalk lines. Dry. Then paint the interiors of the images and designs.
- Draw with markers on individual transparency sheets. Project these images on the wall. Paint the actual wall, tracing the image and filling in with permanent latex paint.

For Budding Artists

- Draw on a large chalkboard with chalk.
- Press hands in paint and make handprints on a large sheet of paper taped to the wall.

Beyond the Wall

Paint a window to the world on a blank wall—an adventurous project that stimulates minds and thrills imaginations of both the artists and art viewers.

Materials

"outside the window" planned view
    (drawing on a
    transparency sheet)
black fine point marker (erasable or
    permanent)
overhead projector

yardstick or other straight edge
pencil or chalk
acrylic paints
paintbrushes
clear spray paint

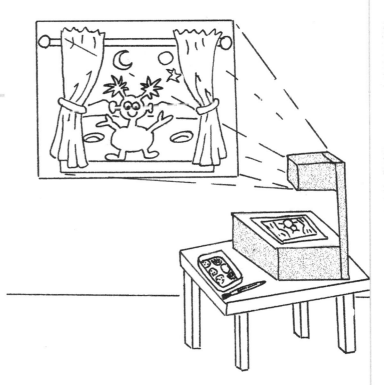

Process

1. Think about a view seen through a window that would make an interesting wall painting. The painting will be projected onto a wall and painted to look like a real window. An outdoor wall, hallway, restroom, and fence all make good surfaces for window-view art. Of course, permission is required for permanent art.
   Some possible themes are:
   - city scene
   - clouds, ocean, alien world
   - dream
   - fine art (copy a famous masterpiece)
   - garden
   - outdoor landscape (pastoral, night)
   - silly or preposterous scene
   - sports activity

2. Draw the window on a blank, clear transparency sheet with a black pen. Begin with a basic window shape. Add choices of curtains, curtain rods, shutters, window trim, sections of glass, objects sitting on the window sill, pot of flowers, and so on (see illustration). Then draw the basic shapes of what will be seen through the window (the view).

3. Place the transparency plan on an overhead projector and shine it on the wall that has been chosen for the painting. With chalk or pencil, trace the black lines directly on the wall. Later, they will be covered with paint, so it doesn't have to be perfect.

4. Set out paints and brushes. Paint sections of the drawing on the wall. Sections may need to dry before adjacent or touching sections are painted. Complete the painting. Let the painting dry for several days. An adult can spray a clear coat of paint over the entire work to protect and allow for soap and water cleaning as needed.

Collage & Assemble

Creativity often consists of merely turning up what is already there. Did you know that right and left shoes were thought up only a little more than a century ago?

—Bernice Fitz-Gibbon,
Macy's advertising executive, (1895–1992)

Breezy Baggies

Melt crayon shavings in wax paper sandwich bags. Transform them into a wispy work of art that moves in air currents and breezes.

Materials

old cheese grater (adult help)	electric warming tray
old crayons	paper towel
newspaper	scissors
work gloves, mittens	hole punch
wax paper sandwich baggies,	plastic hanger
two or more	thread

Process

1. Grate old peeled crayons onto newspaper. Wear work gloves, if preferred, to protect fingers.
2. Pinch together some of the shavings and sprinkle them into a wax paper sandwich baggie. Shake them around to fill the baggie well. Add more, if needed.
3. With adult help, place the baggie on an electric warming tray, allowing the heat to melt the wax paper and the crayon shavings. Press down on the baggie with a gloved hand. Then release.
4. Remove the baggie from the warming tray and see if the baggie has melted together, sealing and laminating the crayon shavings inside. If not, warm a little more, pressing once again. Make at least two melted baggies, or as many as desired.
5. When the baggies have cooled, and the crayon is hard again, cut the baggies into strips or squares. Punch a hole in each one, and tie a thread through the hole. The threads can be different lengths, or all the same. Tie each thread to a plastic hanger, leaving the tie a bit loose so the loop can be moved back and forth to balance. When the pieces are adjusted and balanced, tie the threads tighter.
6. Hang the breezy baggies near a door or window to move as the wind blows gently through the room.

For Budding Artists

- Sprinkle crayon shavings between two layers of wax paper. An adult irons them together at a low temperature to laminate and melt the crayon colors.

Warmed Leaves

Laminated crayon scrapings are transformed into transparent autumn leaves.

Materials

leaves or leaf patterns
white paper (copier paper)
scissors
permanent marker
wax paper
old crayons
old cheese grater
paper plate

paper towels
electric iron (adult only)
tape
choose additional materials, such as:
    glitter, snips of paper doilies,
    sparkly confetti, tiny torn bits of
    aluminum foil, tiny torn bits of foil
    wrapping paper, sequins, other
    shiny sparkly materials

Process

Hint: Leaves are a lovely choice for this art activity, but other shapes, designs, and symbols are equally welcome and creative.

1. Select old crayons in colors that look nice together. Fall colors are a good choice, but other colors can be unique and striking. With adult help, scrape and grate peeled crayon stubs onto a paper plate. Set aside briefly.

2. Trace a leaf or leaf pattern with permanent marker on white paper that has been cut an inch or so larger than the leaf. Cover the leaf tracing with wax paper. The traced leaf outlines will show through the wax paper.

3. Arrange the bits of colored crayon gratings on the wax paper inside the outline of the traced leaf. Add glittery materials for extra sparkle, if desired.

4. When the leaf shape is filled with colorful crayon gratings and sparkles, carefully place a second sheet of wax paper over it. Cover with a paper towel for step 5.

5. With adult help, press the wax paper and crayon gratings firmly with a warm iron, which will melt the crayon and laminate the wax paper sheets together. Cool briefly.

6. Place the laminated crayon and wax paper over the original tracing. Trace the outline on the wax paper with permanent black marker. Cut out the leaf shape from the wax paper. Tape the leaf in a window so the light will shine through and make it glow.

7. Repeat the steps above, creating as many wax paper leaves as desired.

GeoArt

Bright geometric shapes are assembled into a one-of-a-kind design.

Materials

geometrically shaped objects to trace, such as:
- a coaster (circle, other)
- dish (circle)
- jar lids (circles)
- jewelry box (square, rectangle, diamond)
- pre-cut geometric patterns (all)
- miscellaneous items (any shapes)

construction paper scraps, variety of colors

scissors

glue

pencil

Process

1. Trace geometric objects or patterns on construction paper or any variety of colored paper scraps.
2. Cut out the shapes with scissors.
3. Glue the shapes onto a larger piece of construction paper, assembling them to make an object, figure, or pattern of choice.

Shape Idea
- Create art using different sizes of one shape only. For example, art of all circles or all squares.

For Budding Artists

- Glue colorful geometric paper shapes to a background paper.

GeoGram

Work with traditional tangram shapes to create a puzzle, picture, or design.

Materials

choice of scraps or sheets of the following, in any colors, such as:
- construction paper scraps
- felt scraps
- foil wrap or foil craft sheets
- thin foam craft sheets

pencil or marker
ruler
scissors
glue
larger paper for background

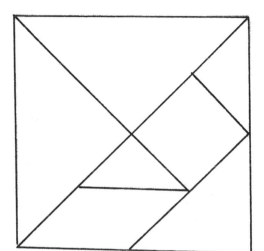

tangram template may be enlarged

Process

1. Draw traditional tangram shapes on one of the colored materials from the list. (See illustration for traditional tangram shapes that fit together in a box-puzzle. Trace these shapes to use as templates, or photocopy to use as a template. The pattern may be reduced or enlarged as needed.)
2. Trace the tangram pieces on colored material. Then cut them out.
3. When the tangram shapes are cut out, assemble them to create a design, shape, figure, or other configuration. Then glue the shapes onto the background paper.

Other Shape Ideas

- Trace a tangram design on plain paper, but only the outline of the whole design, not the edges of each piece. Invite a friend to try to fit tangram shapes into the drawing like a puzzle.
- Combine other geometric or abstract shapes in a design including tangram pieces.
- Use purchased foam shapes (with sticky backing, from craft or school supply stores) instead of drawing and cutting shapes.

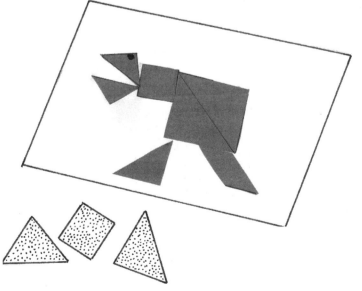

Brain Waves

Express thoughts, wishes, or dreams cascading from an open mind.

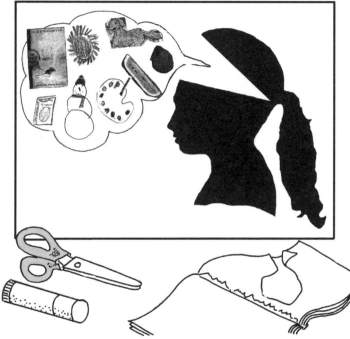

Materials

black paper, or other color choice
pencil or chalk
overhead projector or other strong light source
larger white paper
scissors
glue
magazine pictures, catalog pictures, or small drawings

Process

1. Trace a silhouette of the artist's profile on black paper. To capture a silhouette, the artist should sit next to a wall. Shine an overhead projector or other strong light source until the silhouette is clearly outlined on the wall. Move the black paper to fit over the silhouette, and tape in place. Trace the silhouette with pencil or chalk and cut it out.
2. Cut the top of the silhouette off in a straight line, creating an "open mind." Arrange it so it is open like the top of a hinged jar (see illustration). Glue both pieces on the white background paper.
3. From the opened mind, cut and glue thoughts, wishes, or dreams cascading out across the paper. These can be cut from magazines, catalogs, or selected from small drawings. The thoughts should represent the artist's individual personality and interests.

Photograph Idea

- Enlarge the artist's portrait or school photo on a photocopy machine. Cut the top of the head away in a straight line as in Step 2 above. Glue both pieces on a background paper, as if the mind opened and the artist's thoughts and dreams came pouring out.

For Budding Artists

- Make hand shadows on the wall.
- Draw a person with a cartoon bubble pointing to his or her head, with dreams or thoughts drawn in the bubble.
- Staple several sheets of paper together to make a little book. Draw on each page.

Expressly My Book

Use a board book as the base for creating a unique collage that expresses the artist's personality.

Materials

board book (used book store, dollar store, yard sale)

gesso (art or craft store), one color or more (Gesso is a white paint-like medium that covers print well, offering a new base for artwork. If gesso is not available, simply work on pages as they are.)

glue, tape, stapler

scissors

choices of interesting papers, such as:
crepe paper, foil paper, gift wrap, handmade paper, origami paper, newspaper comics in color, tissue, wallpaper

collage materials, such as:
crinkled paper, embroidery floss, feathers, sequins, shredded paper, string, thin wire, yarn

pictures, such as:
magazines, parts of drawings (cut out), photos, photocopies of photos, stickers

Process

1. Find or purchase a simple board book. Paint each page with gesso to make gluing and painting the pages easier. Some chosen portions and small sections of the original book pages may be left uncovered to show through as part of the new design. Let the pages dry, standing in a fanned-out fashion. Suggestions for decorating the pages include:
   - Coat some of the pages with a solid color or several colors. Choose to let words or pictures show through or remain unpainted.
   - Add collage materials to decorate each page in different ways.
   - Fold, twist, or wrap paper with wire or yarn, or manipulate it in other ways.
   - Cut pictures from a magazine or add photographs to pages. Pictures can represent the artist's personality, hobbies, interests, or feelings.
   - Add individually cut magazine letters or words that further express the artist's uniqueness.

2. Let the glue dry. The final altered book will be an expressive individual work of art.

Additional Book Ideas

- Choose to alter an antiquated textbook, coffee table book, or thick paperback. Consider using a theme in the design, such as patriotism, friendship, sports, careers, or pets.

First Collage

Enjoy an exploratory art activity gluing anything and everything on a sturdy backing.

Materials

paper plate or cardboard for backing
white glue
brush or cotton swab
jar lid
collage materials (see Collage List on page 13)

Process

1. Collect on-hand collage items from the garage, outdoors, or from friends and family. Sort through them, and find those that will be used in a glue-on collage.

   Hint: For collage beginners, limiting a collage to one or two materials helps keep the collage under control. Select combination pairs, such as cotton balls and confetti, or crushed eggshells and foam peanuts.

2. Dip the item in a bit of glue, and then stick it on the paper plate or cardboard backing. Fill the backing with items in any fashion or design. More glue may be squeezed from the bottle if needed, or can be painted onto the item with a brush or cotton swab. Then let the collage dry overnight.

For Budding Artists

- Dip collage items into a little bit of glue and stick them to a paper plate.
- Put glue on a piece of paper and sprinkle confetti or glitter on it to stick.

Inside Out Fancy Collage

Create a fancy collage adding an array of sparkly materials in a pattern that starts in the center and builds its way out to the edges of a cardboard square.

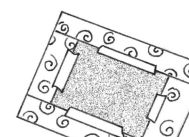

Materials

cardboard square for backing

wrapping paper

tape

choices of collage materials (see Collage List on page 13)

white glue

jar lid

brush

choices of glittery collage materials, such as:

>   beads, bits of aluminum foil, buttons, confetti, Easter grass, glitter, Mylar cut in strips, paper crinkles, plastic bag (shredded), sequins, shiny ribbon

gold, silver, or copper paint, and small paintbrush (optional)

hair spray, or clear acrylic paint (optional)

Process

1. Think fancy and shiny! First, cover a piece of cardboard with wrapping paper. Metallic paper or designs with metallic components work well. Fold the edges of the wrapping paper over the cardboard's edges, and tape on the back.

2. To create the design, begin in the center of the board and work outward. Glue a choice of shiny, fancy materials to the board. Covering the entire board is not necessary. Letting the background paper show through adds to the design.

3. When the collage has dried a bit, take a small paintbrush and lightly highlight the collage with spots and dots of metallic paint. Glue and glitter may also be touched to specific spots for more shine.

4. When everything is dry, an adult can spray the collage with a light coating of hair spray or clear acrylic paint, giving the collage some extra shine and sparkle.

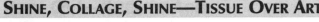

Shine, Collage, Shine

Create a colorful collage with art tissue glued over a shiny foil base and embellished with shiny collage materials.

Materials

colored tissue paper (art tissue)	materials to embellish, such as:	items for hanger:
scissors	glitter, metallic or	metal flip-top lid
poster board	colored thread,	hot glue gun
heavy-duty aluminum foil	sequins, small seed	paper clip
tape	beads, other shiny tiny	duct tape
white glue, container, water	decorations	hole punch
paintbrush		ribbons

Process

1. Cut tissue paper into a variety of large squares, rectangles, or other more abstract shapes.
2. Cover a 10" x 15" (25cm x 35cm) sheet of poster board with heavy-duty aluminum foil (or foiled wrapping paper). Fold over the edges and secure with tape on the back of the poster board.
3. Pour the glue into a container and thin it with water. On the foil side, brush a workable area of the background with glue. Lay tissue shapes into the glue area. Choose to make one layer only, or brush more glue on top of the first layer and add additional layers. After the first area is complete, cover remaining area with foil and add more colorful tissue. Continue until all of the foil is covered with tissue shapes.
4. With tiny dots of glue, embellish the collage with an assortment of shiny delicate materials, such as metallic thread bits, small beads, sequins, glitter or other materials.
5. To make a hanger, choose from several methods:
   - hot-glue a pop-top lid to the back
   - duct tape a paper clip to the back
   - punch holes and suspend by ribbons or yarn

Tissue Quilt Idea
- Cut 4, 9, or 12 paper squares (6" x 6" [15cm x 15cm]). Cover each square with colorful tissue paper cut into typical quilting shapes, such as diamonds, squares, and triangles. Fit them together on the square in a pattern, and then brush them in place with thinned white glue. Repeat the pattern on the other squares. Add additional embellishing materials as described in the main project. Glue all of the quilt squares to a poster board, replicating a quilt.

For Budding Artists

- Brush bright art tissue shapes or scraps onto paper with thinned white glue.

Tissue Over Art

Create a collage with bold patches of colored tissue paper glued over a black line drawing.

Materials

permanent black marker
heavy white paper
colored tissue paper (art tissue)
scissors
white glue, container, water
paintbrush

Process

1. Draw a large, bold picture or design with black marker on heavy white paper. The picture should fill the paper well.

2. Tear or cut tissue paper into shapes, large and small.

3. Brush thinned white glue over part of the drawing. Press tissue paper shapes into the brushed glue, overlapping the pieces some. The drawing will show through the tissue layer. The shapes need not follow the drawing, but instead will extend beyond the outline of the drawing filling the paper with bold patches of color. Brush on more glue and cover the entire drawing with tissue shapes.

4. When the drawing is completely covered, thin a bit of white glue with water and brush lightly to give a smooth shiny finish to the piece. Dry until clear and shiny, usually several hours or overnight.

Art and Color Ideas

- Spell out or design a name, title for the art, message, or poem with letters or words cut from magazines. Then cover with tissue shapes. White tissue is an effective choice in place of colored tissue.

- Color the bold drawing with crayons, markers, or colored pencils, and then cover with tissue.

Basic Collage Drawing

Fill in the spaces of a simple drawing with collage materials, creating texture and color.

Materials

chalk

colorful construction paper or matte board for background

any collage materials, such as:

    beads

    buttons

    cotton balls

    glitter glue

    rickrack

    scraps of paper

    yarn, yarn snips

glue

metallic paint and brush, or metallic pens (optional)

Process

1. Draw a simple bold picture with chalk on colorful background paper; fill the paper well.
2. Fill in the spaces of the drawing with collage materials glued in place.
3. Let the collage dry.
4. For an optional finishing touch, brush metallic paint here and there on the collage drawing adding highlights and sparkle.

For Budding Artists

- Glue collage items on paper, forming a picture or person.
- Draw a shape. Fill the drawing with glue and sprinkle confetti on the glue.

Patterned Paper Picture

Fill in simple drawn shapes with patterned paper bits to create a detailed collage.

Materials

drawing paper

pencil

black marker

glue

scissors

choice of patterned papers, such as:

    catalog pictures

    classified pages

    greeting cards

    magazine pictures

    newspaper comics in color

    wallpaper scraps

    wrapping paper

Process

1. Draw a shape, animal, or other simple object on a sheet of drawing paper. Draw a bold, open design with little detail. More than one shape may be drawn on the paper to create a simple scene or still life.

2. Outline the drawing in black marker.

3. Fill in the spaces in the drawing with snips and bits of wallpaper or other patterned papers. (A good source for wallpaper is discontinued wallpaper books from decorating stores.) Think about how different colors and patterns of paper look best in parts of the drawing.

4. Add other shapes to the paper to make a still life or scene.

Self-Designed Paper Idea

- Create sheets of patterned paper with fingerpainting, doodles, or drawings.

Curious Still Life

Combine tissue paper and a magazine photograph to make a mixed media still life.

Materials

white drawing paper, large background piece	scissors	white glue, dish or lid
pencil	art tissue paper, variety of colors	water
old magazines		paintbrush

Process

This curious still life features the main subject clipped from a magazine. The clipping is incorporated into the surrounding still-life scene. The scene is created from colored tissue.

1. To begin, lightly sketch a still-life scene on the drawing paper with a pencil, leaving out one important part of the drawing. Some examples might be:
   - sketch a table covered with a tablecloth and a pot—ready for flowers to be added.
   - sketch a small table—ready for a bowl of goldfish to sit on it.
   - sketch a patterned pillow on an overstuffed chair—ready for a cat to curl up and nap.
2. Look through an old magazine to find a photograph or picture of the missing still-life subject. (For example, cut out missing flowers to fill the pot that sits on the table, a missing bowl of goldfish to put on the table, or a missing sleeping cat in the overstuffed chair.) Cut out the missing featured part of the still life and glue it into the sketch where it belongs.
3. Look at the different components or pieces of the sketch. Draw each piece separately on different colors of tissue paper. Cut out the pieces and arrange them on the paper in their proper areas. They should cover the main subject.
4. Pour some glue in a small container or lid and add water. Brush over the tissue paper with thinned white glue.
5. When dry, the magazine picture will show through the transparent, colorful tissue.

Photograph Idea
- Work with a photograph of an object, a friend, a family member, or a pet instead of the magazine picture.

For Budding Artists

- Draw a picture of something real, like a vase of flowers or a cat sleeping on a chair.
- Cut a smiling face from a magazine, and glue on paper. Draw a body to go with the face.

Great Art & Me

A photo of oneself becomes part of a newly revised famous work of art!

Materials

print of a famous work of
  great art (from the
  Internet*, printed in color)
Hint: Another good source
of art prints is old
calendars or posters.

photograph of self (or a
  photocopied photograph)
glue
scissors
permanent markers

*These websites have amazing collections
of art images. Explore the Internet to find favorites. There are
thousands!

  Metropolitan Museum of Art—http//:www.metmuseum.org
  National Gallery, London—
    http//:www.nationalgallery.org.uk
  National Gallery of Canada—http//:www.national.gallery.ca
  Museum of Children's Art—http//:www.mocha.org
  Artcyclopedia—http//:www.artcyclopedia.com
  Art.Com—http//:www.art.com
  Artsonia—http//:www.artsonia.com
  Art Sparx—http//:www.artsparx.com
  All Posters—http//:www.allposters.com

Process

1. Find a famous painting on the Internet or elsewhere. The painting should have at least one person or animal in it. Some famous artists' works that are particularly well suited to this project are Rembrandt, Rockwell, Picasso, Blake, Coubert, and Parrish (among many others). Enjoy searching the Internet for great works of art, and choose a favorite.
2. Print the artwork in color, if possible.
3. To become part of the great art, cut around your face in a photograph. Position it in the artwork as the main character, covering the face of the existing subject. A full body cutout may also fit into the painting. It's up to the individual artist to decide how much of the photograph to use.
4. Add more photographs of family members, pets, or friends if they suit the painting.
5. Add more details with permanent markers when the glue has dried.

Photo Idea

- Replace all the characters in a scene with pictures of friends or family.

3-Layer Echelon

Create a three-layer artwork. Mix three techniques—watercolor painting, crayon, and collage.

background

colored paper

painting

Materials

white paper, 4" x 5" (10cm x 15cm)
pencil or marker
scissors
watercolor paints
paintbrush
water
colored paper, 8½" x 11" (20cm x 30cm)
glue
colored paper, bold contrasting color

Process

1. Using a pencil or marker, draw a simple large shape, animal, or object on white paper. Try to fill the paper with the drawn shape, touching all four edges. Use minimal lines and few details.
2. Cut it out and turn it over. Paint with watercolors on this shape.
3. Cut the colored paper into a similar shape, but larger.
4. Glue the first painted shape onto the larger colored paper shape.
5. Glue this pair onto a third, boldly contrasting background paper.

Adding Color and Detail

- Add details to the shapes using colored markers, chalk, or oil pastels. Metallic pens add glowing highlights.

For Budding Artists

- Glue paper scraps on a background paper in any design, leaving spaces between scraps. Glue a second layer of scraps over the first.

Double Trouble Echelon

Mix coloring and cutting in a double image collage.

Materials

2 sheets of white drawing paper, 8½" x 11" (20cm x 30cm)

1 sheet of colored paper, 8½" x 11" (20cm x 30cm)

scissors

crayons

glue

cut two white
shapes at once

cut two colored
shapes at once

Process

1. Fold the white drawing paper in half. Do the same with the colored paper. Set the colored paper aside briefly, and place the white paper on the workspace.

2. To make two identical shapes: Keep the paper folded. Draw a shape on the top layer. Draw it large enough to fill the half, touching all four edges. Cut two shapes from the folded paper at once, following the drawn lines. Color both matching shapes in any way. They may be colored in identical style or in different ways.

3. Place the folded colored paper on the workspace. Trace one of the crayoned shapes on the paper. Cut two shapes at once just as before, following the traced line. Now there are four shapes that are all the same shape, two white and two colored.

4. First glue the colored paper shapes on the unfolded sheet of white drawing paper. Then glue the crayoned shapes overlapping the colored paper shapes.

Additional Color Ideas

• Add details to the shapes with colored markers, oil pastels, or colored chalk.

• Metallic pens effectively highlight chosen areas of the shapes.

Shape Explosion

Assemble a paper collage that appears to have "exploded" into a semblance of itself.

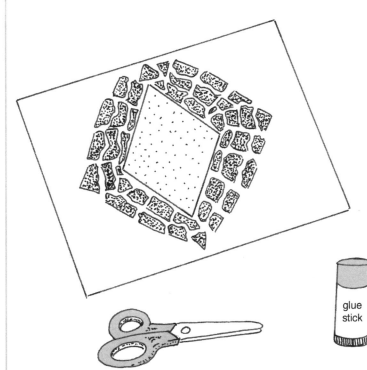

Materials

large sheet of paper for the background (white or black is effective)
two smaller sheets of colored construction paper, any colors
scissors
glue
pencil

Process

1. Draw two identical shapes on the colored construction papers, one on each sheet. The colors may be the same or different.
2. Cut out the shapes.
3. Shape 1: Glue the first shape in the middle of the large background paper. Leave this shape whole.
4. Shape 2: Cut or tear the second shape into smaller pieces. Glue the pieces of the second shape around the whole shape (shape 1), like a broken reflection of itself. (The whole center shape will be surrounded by an explosion of color.)

Color Effects

- **Opposite Color Effect:** Glue small colored pieces of paper on a larger piece of paper in an opposite or contrasting color (for example, glue red shapes on a green background paper, glue yellow shapes on a purple background; glue orange shapes on a blue background).
- **Identical Magazine Effect:** Cut two identical shapes from magazine pictures. Glue one whole shape on the background paper, and tear or cut the second as above.
- **Background Effect:** Choose a used poster or calendar print as the background paper.
- **Word Stripe Effect:** Cut two identical shapes from solid areas of text from a magazine or newspaper. The words can be straight across the design or turned diagonally to create a striped effect. Glue on the classified section of the newspaper as a background.

For Budding Artists

- Glue paper scraps on a background paper in any design, leaving spaces between.
- Color in the squares on large graph paper in any way.

Optigraph

An optical illusion is created with squares of construction paper and sticky dots on a visually twisting layout.

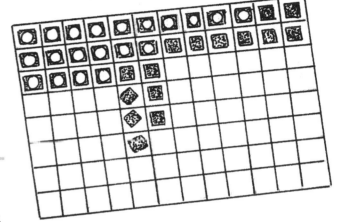

Materials

graph paper, 1" (2.5cm) squares 8½" x 11" (20cm x 25cm) (Graph paper this size
   contains approximately 80–90 squares.)
colored paper
glue stick
sticky dots (stickers in primary colors from office or school supply stores)
black fine-point marker

Process

1. Cut colored paper into approximately 80–90 squares, slightly smaller than one inch—
   about ¾" (2cm).

2. Arrange a selection of colored paper squares in the 1" grid squares on the graph paper.
   Wait to glue them in place. Choose a single color or multiple colors.

Hint: Cut squares in one color for a solid effect, or in several colors for a visually
stimulating effect.

3. When placing the squares, leave a narrow border between all squares. When satisfied
   with the design, glue the squares in place.

4. Press a sticky dot in the center of each square.

Optional: Draw a black line around each square with a fine-point marker.

5. Stand back and enjoy the wild optical effect of color and line.

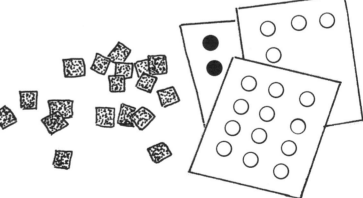

Puzzle Mosaic

Cut a drawing into pieces, and reassemble on a bright background paper, leaving spaces between them, resembling a tile mosaic.

Materials

drawing paper 8 ½" x 11" (20cm x 30cm)

crayons

construction paper (twice the size of the drawing paper)

scissors

glue

Process

1. Draw a picture or design on drawing paper. Color the entire paper, including all background areas. If preferred, also outline all shapes with heavy black crayon.
2. Cut the crayon drawing into as few as six pieces, or as many pieces as can be managed. As the pieces are cut, keep them assembled on the table in picture order.
3. When all the pieces are ready, begin gluing them on a bright background paper. Start with pieces from the center of the drawing, and work outwards to the edges. Leave narrow spaces between the pieces similar to the look of tiles.
4. Let the work dry for an hour.

Rubbing Idea

● For extra art fun, make a rubbing of the mosaic. Place a sheet of drawing paper over the mosaic, and then rub the drawing paper with a peeled crayon on its side to pick up the shapes of the cut pieces.

For Budding Artists

● Draw a picture and cut it into four or more strips. Glue it back together on a background paper.

Foil Shimmer Mosaic

Aluminum foil is transformed by a mixture of glue and food coloring into shimmery faux tiles used to create a distinctive mosaic.

Materials

white glue

food coloring (or Liquid Watercolors™)

aluminum foil squares, approximately 6" x 6" (15cm x 15cm),
   one square for each color desired

paintbrush

sponge brush

scissors

black construction paper

white glue in a squeeze bottle

Process

1. Make a puddle of white glue and food coloring on a square of aluminum foil. Adjust the ratio of food coloring to glue to get the level and intensity of color desired.

2. Spread the colored glue in a thin layer over the sheet of aluminum foil with the sponge brush. Make several more squares of foil and glue. Let all the squares dry overnight.

Hint: A thin layer of glue works best; thick glue is too heavy for step three.

3. When the glue on the foil is completely dry, cut the colorful foil into small pieces with scissors, creating pieces that look like colorful tiles or jewels. Create squares, diamonds, triangles, and any other shapes of choice.

4. Glue the mosaic pieces onto black construction paper to create a free-form design. (If preferred, pre-draw a picture with pencil on the black paper. Then glue the foil pieces into place.)

Plaster Mosaic

Create a whimsical mosaic with found objects embedded in a plaster of Paris base.

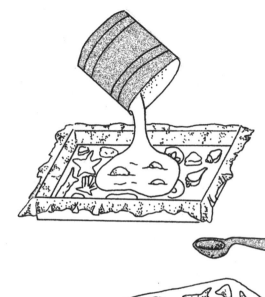

Materials

	choice of found objects, such as:		
gift box			
aluminum foil	beach glass	craft jewels	plastic silverware
plaster of Paris	beads	gadgets	shells
coffee can	Bingo markers	game pieces	small tiles
water	broken toy parts	leather scraps	smooth stones
stirring stick	buttons	nuts and bolts	straws
food coloring	coins	old silverware	tiddly winks
(optional)	colorful plastic caps	pebbles	washers
plastic spoon	colorful plastic lids	pieces of tiles	wood chips

Process

1. Line the bottom of a box with foil, pressing it into the corners.
2. Cover the bottom of the box with found items in a pattern or design.

Hint: Turn the best side of each object towards the bottom, as this is the side that will eventually show.

3. Fill a coffee can half-full with plaster of Paris. Add water, quickly stirring until the mixture looks like heavy cream (food coloring may be added at this step if colored plaster is preferred). Pour the plaster over the items in the box just enough to cover them completely. Quickly smooth plaster with a plastic spoon.
4. Allow the plaster to dry, usually from 30 minutes to 1 hour.
5. Gently tear away the box, and carefully peel away the foil. Turn the plaster mosaic over, and see the found objects facing out in their arranged design.
6. Let the plaster mosaic rest overnight until fully dry. Display on a table or shelf.

Hint: Do not rinse plaster down the drain or a serious clog may occur. Allow the plaster to dry, then crumble and place in the trash or garden.

For Budding Artists

- Glue squares of paper in a design on a cardboard background.
- Press tile squares into playdough or clay. Air dry.

True Tile Mosaic

Create a permanent mosaic that is remarkably authentic. Small tiles are arranged on a plywood base using a combination commercial mix called "adhesive-grout." The final artwork is permanent and weather resistant.

Materials

assorted small tiles and pieces of tiles (from stores with home décor, building supply, tile, or crafts)

square of plywood (any size, from small to large) or cardboard*

tub of "adhesive-grout combination mixture"

spatula or putty knife

serrated plastic spoon (sometimes called a "spork"), or a small serrated trowel

old towel

bucket of warm water

*Instead of plywood or cardboard, choose to cover a clay pot, the top of an old garden bench, a birdbath, or other suitable outdoor garden surface to create a permanent outdoor decoration.

Process

1. Practice arranging tiles on the plywood. When satisfied with the design, place the tiles beside the board.
2. Spread adhesive-grout on the plywood with a spatula. Go over with a serrated spoon or trowel to rough the texture.

Hint: Spread adhesive grout in small areas because it remains soft and workable for 10 to 30 minutes after spreading, allowing an opportunity to adjust the tile design.

3. Arrange tiles in the adhesive-grout to form the practiced pattern. Leave a little space between tiles. Adjust tiles before adhesive hardens. After that, the tiles will be permanent. Wipe off extra adhesive-grout with a damp rag. Rinse rag in a bucket of warm water.
4. Continue to apply adhesive and tiles, completing the design.
5. To finish, spread adhesive-grout between all tiles with a broad spatula or putty knife. Smooth and spread, wiping excess from tiles with the spatula while working. Wipe off excess adhesive-grout with a clean damp rag. Rinse rag often. Keep wiping until the tiles look thoroughly cleaned of grout.
6. Let dry at least 30 minutes for a soft dry, or overnight for a completely hard dry. When dry, polish the tiles to a shine with a clean damp rag.

Broken Dinnerware Idea

Old dinnerware makes interesting mosaic pieces. Always wear safety goggles when breaking tile or dishware. Use caution: broken edges can be sharp. To break into pieces, cover the piece of dinnerware or plate with an old towel. Hammer gently to break into large pieces. For smaller pieces, continue hammering and breaking pieces gently.

Safety Note: Adult help, supervision, and guidance is essential for all the steps in the process.

Wavy Collage Weave

Strips of construction paper are torn and then glued on bright wrapping paper in a simulated weaving design.

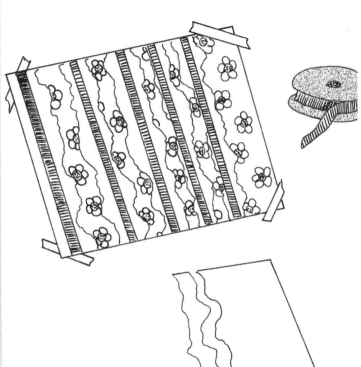

Materials

construction paper, about 12" x 12" (30cm x 30cm)

gift wrap paper (patterned designs work best), about 12" x 12" (30cm x 30cm)

tape

glue

ribbon (If preferred, substitute ribbon with yarn, embroidery floss, or other colorful strands)

scissors

Process

1. Spread a square piece of gift wrap paper on the worktable. Tape the corners to the table for stability.
2. Tear a square of construction paper into strips of any width. Tear each strip slowly, pinching and tearing little bits at a time.
3. Glue the strips on the gift wrap all in a row, spreading them out and leaving space between them.
4. While this dries, cut ribbon into 12" (30cm) lengths.
   Glue a strip of ribbon to the center of each construction paper strip.
5. Dry well. Gently pull tape from the table. Trim extra tape from the paper's corner.

For Budding Artists

• Tear any paper into strips and glue on a construction paper background.

• Glue squares of paper in a pattern on a background paper.

Counterfeit Weave

Glue large, colorful paper squares on a contrasting background in a simulated weaving pattern.

Materials

large sheet of construction paper (for background)
construction paper (one color or many colors)
scissors
glue stick

Process

1. Cut construction paper into 2″ (5cm) squares, using one color or many.
2. Glue one square anywhere on the construction paper background.
3. Next, glue another square, making sure that one of its corner points touches a corner point of the first square (see illustration).
4. Keep adding squares with points touching, forming a checkerboard-style design.
5. When the squares are glued and the design is complete, it will resemble a random over-under weaving in pattern and design.

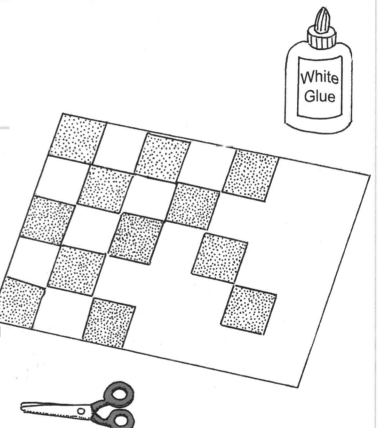

Embellishment Ideas

- Cut a second group of 2″ (5cm) squares from metallic or foil paper. Intersperse the foil squares with the colored squares.
- Fill in the blank square shapes with glitter glue.
- Trace square shapes with glitter glue.
- Place a small decorative sticker in each colored paper square.
- Use paper rectangles or diamond shapes.

Image Interweave

A used, colored file folder becomes a starter loom (the warp). Generate a picture weaving (the weft) from an outdated calendar picture to create a weaving with captivating results.

"Stop cutting" line

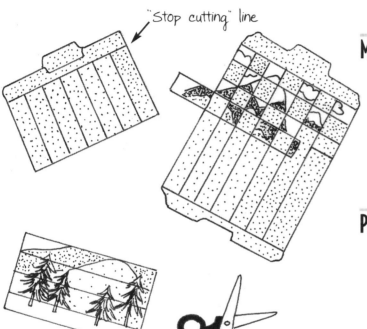

Materials

old colored file folders, two (in any color)
ruler
pencil
scissors
outdated calendar with large images
glue
tape

Process

1. Measure and draw a line within 1" (3cm) of the open edge of a colored file folder (see illustration). The 1" (3cm) line is the "stop cutting here" guide. Draw lines spaced about 2" (6cm) in width from the folded edge up to this line at the open edge. This file folder will be called the "warp."

2. Cut on the drawn lines, stopping at the line drawn near the open edge. The open folder becomes a loom ready for weaving.

Hint: Cutting on the lines will give a straight weaving. Using the lines as a guide and cutting wavy or zigzag lines will give a pop-art style of weaving.

3. Select a large picture from an outdated calendar. When cut, this will be called the "weft." Trim the image to a size slightly smaller than the open folder. Glue it to a second file folder to give it some weight and strength. When the glue has dried some, cut the calendar picture into 2" (6cm) strips, keeping them in order.

4. Weave each weft strip (the calendar strips), one at a time, in an over-under pattern through the file folder warp strips. Each strip should be slid snuggly to the next for a tight weave that highlights the assembled calendar picture strips. Secure loose edges of calendar (weft) strips with a dot of white glue or a bit of tape.

5. When the entire folder is filled, the result will be a visually stimulating pictorial weaving. Stare at the weaving. It may appear to be moving, a visual trick the brain and eyes play on each other.

For Budding Artists

- Cut a painting into strips or shapes and glue them on a background paper in any design.
- Weave paper through yarn wrapped around and around a cardboard square.

Woven Watercolor

Cut two spattered watercolor paintings into strips and loosely weave them together.

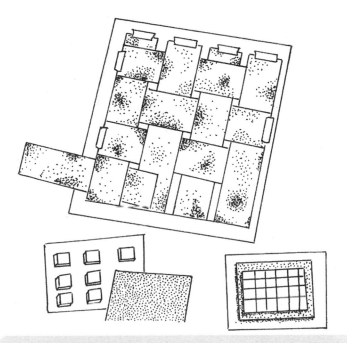

Materials

watercolor paper or other heavy paper,
   approximately 9" x 12" (20cm x 30cm)
watercolor paints and brushes
dish of water
scissors
stiff paper backing for weaving 9" x 12"
   (20cm x 30cm)

tape and glue
8–12 chunks of Styrofoam, 1" (2cm) square
large matte board, 11" x 17"
   (30cm x 40cm)
foam core or matte board, 9" x 12"
   (20cm x 30cm)

Process

1. Spatter a heavy sheet of paper with watercolor paints. Spatter a second sheet with a similar pattern or with all new colors and designs. Set both aside to dry.

2. Cut each spattered paper lengthwise into 3" to 4" (8cm to 10cm) strips. Keep the strips from each painting separated into two stacks.

3. Arrange one set of four strips vertically (up and down) on the stiff paper backing. These strips are the "warp." Lightly tape the top end of each warp strip, one next to the other in a row, with edges slightly apart. Strips do not need to be in their original order.

4. Begin with one strip from the second stack. The strips that weave in and out are the "weft." Starting "over," or on top of the warp, weave one strip horizontally (left to right, or right to left) through the warp strips in an **over-under** pattern. Leave spaces for a loose weave. Weave the weft strip completely through the warp, and tape to hold.

5. Weave the next weft strip, this time starting under the warp in an **under-over** pattern. Tape the ends when done. Then complete the weaving with the remaining strips.

6. When all the weft strips are woven through the warp, tape all loose ends to the backing. To cover the tape, tear or cut any leftover spattered paper into squares or strips and glue over the taped areas of the weaving.

Three-Dimensional Display Board

Glue 4–6 Styrofoam chunks (about 1" [2cm] square) spaced evenly on a foam core board (or matte board). Glue and center a second matte board onto these four chunks. The second matte board will be raised off the first. Let dry while working on the next step. Glue 4–6 more Styrofoam chunks spaced evenly on the back of the weaving. Then glue the weaving to the layers of matte board. The weaving will be raised away from the matte, and the matte will be raised from foam core, rendering a three-dimensional display technique. Layer the pieces from largest (on the bottom), mid-size matte board (in the middle), to the slightly smaller weaving (on the top).

Tube Time

Create a soft sculpture to bend and twist into a shape.

Materials

strip of muslin, approximately 12" x 36" (⅓m x 1m)
tacky glue or sewing machine
wire, medium weight, 36" (1m)
fiberfill stuffing
yarn
stapler
ruler or yardstick
choice of paints (in squeeze bottles or with paintbrush) such as:
    acrylic paints, fabric paints, liquid watercolors, puffy paints
variety of scraps and pieces for decorating, including:
    buttons, colorful thread, fabric scraps, felt, leather, ribbons, sequins, sewing trims
pushpin, tack, or picture hanger

Process

1. With adult help, fold the strip of muslin the long way with right sides together. Sew or glue the muslin strip down the long side. If using glue, dry until the glue holds well. Then turn the strip right side out. The rough seams of the tube will be inside the tube.
2. Tie one end closed with yarn.
3. Insert the wire into the length of the tube, and bend ends into small loops. Holding the wire to one side, stuff the tube full with fiberfill stuffing. A ruler or yardstick will help stuff the tube. To close, tie the open end with yarn, glue, or staple.
4. Paint the tube with any choices of paints. Use squeeze bottles, or apply with a paintbrush. Paints may also be spattered or sprayed on the tube. Glue other scraps and bits of materials on the tube to further decorate and add highlights of color, texture, and design. Then allow the paint to dry.
5. Bend or twist the tube into a desired shape, such as a knot, circle, V, wiggle, or wave.
6. Pin the shaped tube to a board, hang it from a pushpin or picture hanger on the ceiling, or stick the tube to the wall with a pushpin.

Multiple-Tubes Weaving Idea

- Make two, three, or more tubes. Form into initials, a name, or a short word.

For Budding Artists

- Paint with watercolor paints on fabric.
- Work yarn through the holes in a plastic berry basket to create a weaving.

Enormous Group Weave

Work together to build a tube weaving on an open wall space.

Materials

muslin fabric, 12" x 36" (⅓m x 1m)
masking tape
fabric paints
sewing machine (with adult help), or needle and thread
fiberfill
ruler or yardstick
elastic, from sewing or hobby shop, about 12 yards (15m)
pushpins or stapler
bulletin board

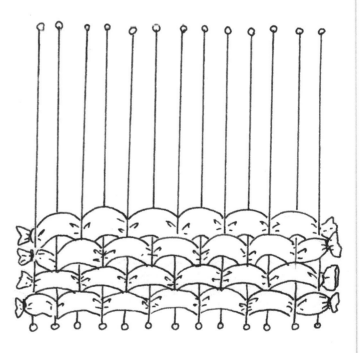

Process

1. Each artist will need a wide strip of muslin. Spread it on the table. Tape here and there to hold. Paint the muslin with fabric paints. Let dry. Then remove tape.

2. With adult help, fold the muslin strip in half the long way, and sew the long edge of folded strip with right sides together to form a tube. Turn so right sides are out. Stuff tube with fiberfill, pushing the stuffing in with a ruler or a yardstick. Tie off ends with yarn using double knots (see illustration).

3. String elastic vertically on a large bulletin board, sheet of plywood, or open wall, using pushpins or staples. These vertical strips form the warp threads (the loom for the weaving). Warp threads should be about 3" or more apart.

4. Working as a group, each artist weaves a tube (the weft) over and under the elastic (the warp) to make an enormous weaving. Tie off the warp elastic on the ends. The weaving may be removed from the wall and moved and displayed anywhere.

Hint: Additional pins or staples may be added for support, if elastic or tubes sag.

Color Idea

● Work with colors in the weaving to go with a chosen theme, such as:
  spring, holiday, undersea, outer space, rain forest, or patriotism.

Circle Burst

Create a bright weaving on the metal lid of a juice can. String materials through holes punched around its edge.

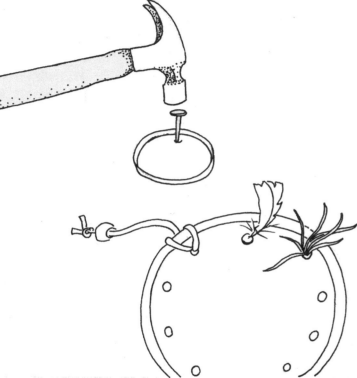

Materials

metal top saved from frozen juice container
choice of color (optional), including:
    fabric paints (in squeeze bottle or with a brush)
paint and paintbrush
permanent markers
choice of collage materials for weaving, including:
    beads, feathers, raffia, ribbon, string, thin strips of paper, twist-ties, yarn
hammer
nail
wooden board to protect table
work gloves
safety goggles

Process

1. With adult help and supervision, punch holes around the edge of a metal juice container lid with hammer and nail. Working on a wooden board will protect the table and keep the lid from bending. Wear work gloves to help protect fingers and safety goggles to protect eyes.
2. Paint or decorate the lid, or leave as is (shiny and metallic).
Hint: Permanent markers decorate metal very well, allowing some of the shine to remain.
3. To add materials to the circle burst, push and string them through the holes in any fashion, either random or planned.
Hint: Beads can be strung on the strings or pieces of yarn that are woven through the lid, adding design and interest.

Other Circle Burst Ideas
- cardboard pizza circle (hammer/nail)
- plastic container from salad bar, cut lid into a circle (hole punch)
- plastic coffee can lid (hole punch)

For Budding Artists

- Wrap yarn through slits cut in the edges of a rectangle of cardboard.
- Sew yarn through a Styrofoam grocery tray with pre-poked holes.

Rich Hoop Basket

Weave long strips and strings through interlocking hoops.

Materials

choice of base material to make hoops, each strand or strip about 24" to 36" (60cm to 90cm) long, such as:
- 3–4 strips of railroad board or poster board (about 1" [2cm] wide) (will need a stapler)
- 3–4 coffee can plastic lids, centers cut away (will need scissors and adult help and supervision)
- 3–4 wires (will need wire cutters or shears)

3–4 stiff cords (will need scissors)
3 embroidery hoops
scissors
pushpin or picture hanger
choices of materials to weave, such as:
- corn husks, fabric strings or strips, grape vine, lace, long grasses, long pine needles, plastic lacing, raffia, ribbon, rickrack, sea grass, surveyor tape, torn strips of fabric

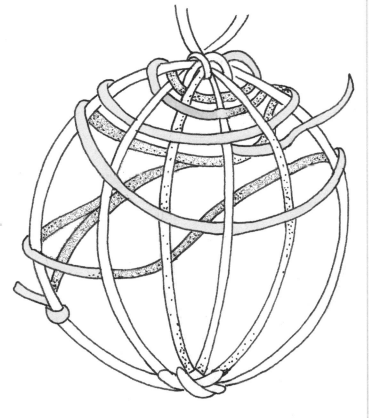

Process

1. Bend a 24" to 36" (60cm to 90cm) long strand of railroad board, wire, or cord into a hoop. Make three or four round hoops. (The easiest method is to make 3 to 4 strips of railroad board or other stiff paper, and staple them to form hoops.)
2. Interlock the hoops by slipping one inside another, spacing them to form a sphere (see illustration).
3. Weave longer strands of materials, back and forth through the hoops.

Hint: Attach the hoops to a closed doorknob or the back of a chair to hold the hoop steady during weaving. Weave gently, being careful not to crush the hoop shape.

4. Weave in more materials until the hoops are full of color and texture. Weave both horizontally and vertically. Change materials often for a varied outcome.
5. Display the hoop weaving from a piece of string or wire hanging from a pushpin or picture hanger in the ceiling or from the window casing.

Weaving Ideas
- Attach beads, feathers, short pieces of ribbon, Mylar strips, or tinsel throughout the weaving.
- Tie mementos or small souvenirs that express a theme, such as to express a "memory weaving" or a "friendship weaving."

Fabric Pot

Cover a terra cotta pot with overlapping scraps of fabric coated with permanent gloss.

Materials

1 terra cotta clay pot, any size
paintbrushes
newspapers
clear hobby coating, such as Modpodge™
fabric scraps, patterned (cut in strips and squares)
scissors
sewing trim or braid, enough to go around the top of the pot

Process

1. Make a pad of newspapers several layers thick for a workspace. Place the pot upside down on the pad.
2. With a paintbrush dipped in clear hobby coating, stick the fabric pieces onto the pot little by little, one piece at a time. Press out wrinkles with fingers and the brush. Overlap pieces so the pot surface does not show. Work until the sides and bottom of the pot are fully covered. The top edge or rim must wait until the pot is dry. Dry for several hours or overnight.
3. Turn the pot over. Finish sticking fabric scraps with clear hobby coating on the rim of the pot, overlapping the scraps into the inside of the pot.
4. Add a piece of sewing trim to the pot's collar for the final touch. Dry completely.

For Budding Artists

- Glue magazine scraps to a block of wood. Brush over them with more glue.
- Make a 3-D collage by gluing objects on a block of wood.

Gesso Collection Box

Create a special box to hold special things.

Materials

school box or cigar box

gesso* (primer base from any art or craft store)

sponge paintbrush

acrylic paint

other paintbrushes

craft glue

choice of collectibles, such as:

    collage materials or collected items

    natural items (stones, shells, pressed flowers)

    photographs (interesting parts cut out or used whole)

    special items (old small toys, old jewelry, sports cards)

*Gesso is a white primer that helps the box accept glue, paint, and other mediums. If gesso is not available, paint the box with acrylics without the gesso coat.

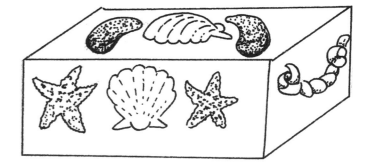

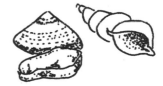

Process

1. Peel off the paper from the school box or cigar box.
2. Paint the box with gesso. Allow it to dry for 1–2 hours.
3. Paint the box with any chosen color of acrylic paint. When the color is dry, put on a second coat. Then dry. The paint must be completely dry for step four.
4. Decorate the box with any choice of collectibles on the lid or sides. More designs may also be painted at this time. Let the glue and paint dry. Keep special collectibles in the collection box, or give as a gift to someone special with something special tucked inside.

Sink or Float Boat

Will it sink or will it float? Assemble a floating collage on a block of Styrofoam, and take the floating test!

Materials

flat block or sheet of Styrofoam
hammer, mallet, or block of wood
scissors

choice of materials to decorate, such as:
    bamboo skewers
    craft sticks
    drinking straws
    golf tees
    plastic bags cut in strips or squares
    ribbons
    rubber bands
    Styrofoam grocery trays, cut in shapes
    toothpicks
    yarn, string, or ribbon
    other chosen recyclable items

Process

1. Place the block of Styrofoam on the work surface. Turn it over to see which way is most stable and would float best.
2. Begin decorating the boat, keeping the word "balance" in mind. (The weight should be equally balanced so the boat won't tip to one side or overturn.) Push or hammer items deep into the Styrofoam, but not all the way through. Add yarn, string, and ribbon to blow in the wind. Sails can be made from plastic bags cut to size. Decorate with any style or ideas.
3. Will the boat sink or float? Place the boat in a tub, wading pool, sink, or even a puddle to find the answer. If the boat tips or seems overweight, adjust the "cargo" until it floats successfully.

For Budding Artists

- Float and sink a variety of objects in water.
- Make a collage by gluing objects on a block of wood.

Watery World

Transform an old fish aquarium into a visually intriguing watery art experience.

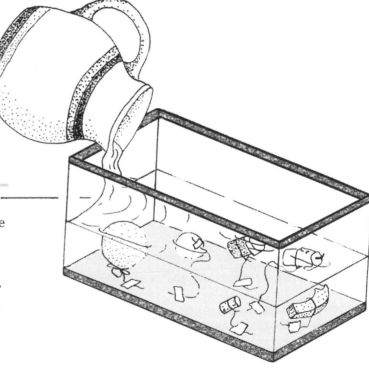

Materials

objects that float, such as:
> balloons filled with air and tied to hold, corks (all sizes), film canisters (lids on), foam peanuts, lids of plastic bottles, plastic bottles (small), pieces of Styrofoam, ping-pong balls, small candles, small hollow toys, wooden chunks or small blocks

deep bowl of water for testing
towel

old fish aquarium (dry), 5 gallon size (20 liters, approximately)
fishing line or heavy thread (colored embroidery floss is effective)
duct tape, other tape, glue (hot-glue gun adult only), stapler
scissors
water to fill aquarium, pitcher or container for pouring
food coloring (optional)
gravel or aquarium gravel

Process

1. Find household objects and toys that should float. Test each one in a deep bowl of water to be sure. Only floating objects will work. (It is fine if objects sink a little but are suspended off the bottom of the bowl.) Select objects and dry well.

2. Cut one strand of fishing line or heavy thread for each object in different lengths, no longer than the height of the fish aquarium (approximately 12" [30cm]) or shorter. Tie, glue, staple, or otherwise attach a strand of fishing line or heavy thread to each object selected. (A hot-glue gun is a waterproof-dependable method for this project.) Then, with hot-glue (adult only) or duct tape, attach the empty end of the line or thread securely to the bottom of the aquarium. All objects will be on the bottom of the aquarium.

3. Gently scoop aquarium gravel into the tank to cover the bottom, hiding tape and glue and adding color and texture.

4. Very gently pour water into the aquarium. Keep adding water until the aquarium is almost full. As the water fills, the objects will float. Depending on the length of the line or thread, some objects will be submerged and others will float to the surface. Add food coloring to color the water, if desired.

5. Enjoy watching the objects floating in the watery world.

To the Letter Collage

Browse outdated magazines for artsy letters to snip and paste into an overlapping collage image.

Materials

materials with large printed letters and words, appropriate for cutting, such as:
    catalogs, magazines, newspapers, cereal boxes, soup and other food labels, junk mail
containers to hold cutouts
scissors
stiff paper for the background, such as:
    cardboard, matte board, paper plate (heavy), poster board
glue
white glue, container, water
paintbrush

Process

1. Browse through old magazines, searching for large alphabet letters and fancy large words.
2. Cut out favorite letters and words and keep on a paper plate or in a shoe box.
3. When ready, begin gluing the letters on the background paper, overlapping them to completely cover the background.
4. Place some of the words over some of the letters and glue in place.
5. When the collage is complete, brush over the entire collage with a layer of white glue thinned with water to seal it and add shine.

Letter Collage Ideas
- Select letters that spell out a name, title, or message.
- Select many different font designs featuring the same letter of the alphabet.
- Find all the letters of the alphabet.
- Combine matching letters and pictures in an alpha-match collage.

For Budding Artists

- Cut pictures and letters from a magazine or catalog and glue on paper.
- Cut a hole in a sheet of paper and glue on a contrasting paper.

Peekaboo Collage

What's behind doors 1, 2, and 3? Take a peek to see the hidden collage images.

Materials

scissors

materials with bright pictures, appropriate for cutting, such as:
    catalogs, magazines, newspaper comics in color

stiff paper for background, approximately 20" wide x 15" tall (50cm wide x 80cm tall),
    such as matte board, cardboard, poster board, foam core board

glue

construction paper squares, in any color or colors

tray to hold cutouts

tape

white glue, container, water

paintbrush

Process

1. Cut or tear selections from catalogs and magazines.
2. Cover the entire background paper with the magazine clippings. Let them overlap so the entire background is covered. Glue in place. Set aside to dry briefly while completing the next step.
3. Cut construction paper into squares approximately 5" x 5" (10cm x 10cm). Fold each paper square in half. Cut a shape into the folded side of the square. Remove the shape and set outside. Unfold the square. Do this for each square. The shapes cut into the squares can be the same or different.
4. Glue all the squares (not the cut-away shapes) side by side on the collage, covering the entire collage (see illustration). There is now a two-layer collage, with magazine clippings showing through the holes in the squares.
5. To make peekaboo doors, position each cut-away shape in its proper space. Tape one side of the shape only, forming a hinge that will let the shape open and close.
6. Gently close the collage "doors." Display so art viewers may peek inside.

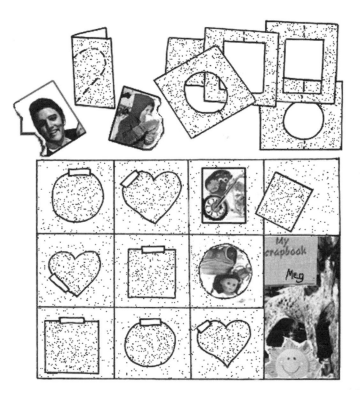

Peekaboo Ideas

- Glue a deliberate cutout image under each door to surprise viewers, like a cute puppy, pretty flower, or silly monkey.
- Glue words, letters, pictures, or stickers on the outside of each door.

Sculpt & Construct

There is no 'must' in art because art is free.

—Wassily Kandinsky, artist (1866–1944)

Big Bag Sculpture

Create a large floppy bag sculpture filled with packing peanuts.

Materials

plastic garbage bag (clear is attractive, but any color is fine), large size for lawns and gardens

packing peanuts, or other lightweight filler material

stapler

string, yarn, or masking tape

scissors

materials for embellishment, such as:

    colored paper

    colorful art tissue

    cotton balls

    feathers

    ribbons

Process

1. Fill a plastic garbage bag half full with packing peanuts or other lightweight filling. Shake the bag to help the peanuts spread throughout the bag. Push the air out. Staple or tie the opening closed.

2. Squeeze and move the peanuts around inside the bag, forming areas that are full of peanuts, and areas that are empty or almost empty. Tie off sections with yarn, string, or tape to sculpt the bag into a shape with many parts and sections. Yarn and tape can also be used to make the sculpture stay upright or hold a position.

3. Add materials of choice to embellish and decorate. Some ideas are:
   - cut colored paper scraps into designs and tape to the bag
   - tie colored ribbons to the bag; ribbons can be curled
   - tape feathers, cotton balls, or other collage items to the bag
   - cut colorful art tissue into shapes or strips and tape to the bag

For Budding Artists

- Draw a face on a lunch bag and stuff it with newspaper.
- String cereal on yarn to make a snack necklace.

Festive Festoon

Create a very long garland on yarn made with sections of drinking straws and packing peanuts.

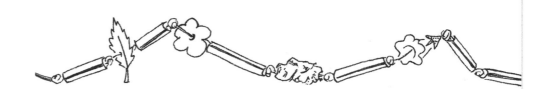

Materials

drinking straws or coffee stirrers (restaurant supply, discount store)
yarn (skein, ball, or long strands)
masking tape
scissors
decorating materials, such as:
    aluminum foil
    plastic flowers and leaves
    shapes of colorful art tissue, cut or torn
    wax paper shapes, cut or torn
packing peanuts
yarn, shorter pieces about 6" (15cm) long

Process

1. Cut drinking straws into three or four sections. Cut a handful all at once, but cut them inside a paper bag to keep them from flying around the room. Prepare many straws to make this garland a truly festive festoon...and a long one at that!

2. Tape the end of a piece of yarn to form a pointed "stringing needle." Push the tape needle through a straw and out the other end. Slide the straw all the way to the other end of the piece of yarn. Then tie a knot or make a knotted loop. Tie a knot each time the yarn comes through a straw so that the straws don't slip.

3. Between straw sections, string an item on the yarn, such as:
   - art tissue cut in flower shapes or geometric shapes
   - plastic flowers or leaves
   - wax paper shapes
   - aluminum foil squeezed around yarn or threaded

4. With colorful short pieces of yarn, tie packing peanuts to the garland. Tie securely but not so tight that the packing peanuts crumble.

5. Create a festive garland that wraps around the entire room and back.

6. Hang the festive festoon in a draping fashion. The straws will cause the garland to take on its own form where each straw joins the next.

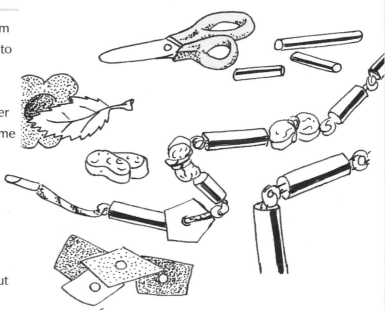

Rock On!

Sculpt a life-size reproduction of a rock made from newspaper, tape, and plaster cloth.

Materials

newspaper

masking tape

plaster cloth (craft stores, pharmacy) or gauze strips (pharmacy) dipped in
    wet plaster of Paris

tempera paints

sponges

paintbrushes

Process

1. To create "rocks," wad up several sheets of newspaper into a rock shape. Wrap the paper rock with masking tape to give it a hard form.

2. Dip plaster cloth strips in water according to the instructions on the box, pressing out extra water with fingers. (An alternative idea is to dip gauze in plaster of Paris and wipe off excess plaster mix with fingers.) Cover the tape-wrapped "rocks" with the plaster cloth strips. Dry completely.

3. Dip sponges in tempera paint and blot and dab the paint onto the rock to give it a textured look. To appear most rock-like, first sponge on one layer of one color and let dry. Follow this with a second layer in a different color dabbed on more lightly. Allow paint to dry completely.

Paint Ideas

- speckled—layer gray, then white, then black
- sandstone—layer yellow, tan, then cream
- striped—layer colors of choice; when dry, add streaks of black or white

4. As an optional idea, paint a petroglyph design on the rock. Look in books for ideas, or create unique designs that represent the artist's personality or interests. Initials and names are good choices.

For Budding Artists

- Scrunch aluminum foil into balls.

Rock of Ages

Make a replica of a slab of ancient rock with etchings and designs embedded in the surface.

Materials

Styrofoam sheet, approximately 10" x 10" x ½" (25cm x 25cm x 2cm),
   or any manageable size
light tan or light gray spray paint (rock color)
pencil or paintbrush handle
brown or black acrylic paint, or other color choices
paintbrushes
rag
jar of water for rinsing brushes

Process

1. To make the flat rock: Break away chunks from the sides of a Styrofoam sheet to create rough, irregular edges.
2. An adult can spray the surface of the chunks lightly with beige or gray spray paint in a well-ventilated area. Let dry.
3. To carve the flat rock: With a pencil or a paintbrush handle, dig and etch designs and shapes into the painted Styrofoam chunks. Designs may be random, or may imitate petroglyphs (carvings in rock) and rock paintings.
4. Next, brush brown or black paint inside the lines and designs to make them more visible. Other colors of paint may be used if preferred.
5. To give the rocks an ancient look, wipe brown or black paint with a rag on the sides of the Styrofoam.

Foil Squeezy

Squeeze foil into long snake shapes that can be further bent into abstract shapes. Attach shapes to each other with masking tape. Tape the joined foil sculpture to a square of cardboard to display.

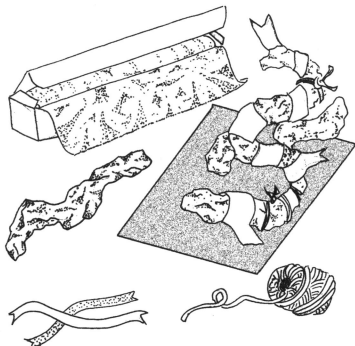

Materials

heavy-duty aluminum foil, about 3' (1m) long

masking tape

cardboard square or matte board

metallic gift ribbon (optional)

scissors

Process

1. Pull a large sheet of aluminum foil from the roll, and tear it off. Tear this sheet into three or four more long sections.
2. Squeeze each section into a long snake shape.
3. Bend and squeeze the shapes into abstract forms, joining them together with masking tape.
4. When completed, tape the joined foil sculpture onto a square of cardboard or matte board.

Hint: Tie and wrap metallic ribbons around the sculpture for added color and shine.

For Budding Artists

- Scrunch aluminum foil into balls and snakes.
- Scrunch newspaper into balls and rolls.

Foil Figure

Squeeze and bend aluminum foil in the shape of a person or figure, wrap in masking tape, and add paint and decorations to create hair and clothing.

Materials

aluminum foil

masking tape

acrylic paint and brush (or colored permanent markers)

glue

decorations and embellishments, such as:

    confetti

    crinkled paper

    fabric

    feathers

    wiggle eyes

    sequins

    yarn

additional props (optional)

scrap matte board

hot glue gun (optional, adult only)

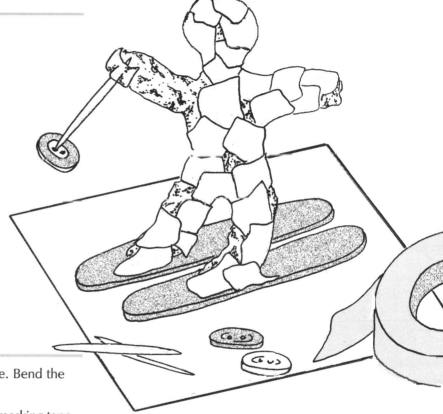

Process

1. Scrunch, crumple, and bend aluminum foil into a human or animal shape. Bend the figure into a pose or posture.

2. Wrap the figure in masking tape to cover. Tear small pieces and strips of masking tape to cover the entire figure.

3. Add details such as facial features and expression to the figure with acrylic paint or colored permanent markers. Glue pieces of yarn, fabric, sequins, and other decorations to create clothing and hair. Additional props can also be added to express more about the figure, such as a ball, tiny toys, or items that are found on key chains.

4. Place the matte board flat on the tabletop. Attach the sculptured person to the matte board with tape. Add enough tape for the person to stand and be strong! (If necessary, use a hot-glue gun with adult supervision.)

Loopty Doo-It

Create patterned paper strips that curl and loop around a cardboard tube, producing a visually exciting and amusing structure.

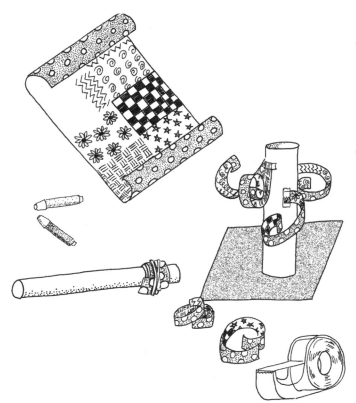

Materials

gift wrap, on a roll (pattern on one side only)	scissors	cardboard square
permanent black marker, medium point	dowel, paintbrush handle, or broom handle	tape, any variety
ruler	rubber band	stapler
	paper towel tube	scissors

Process

1. Spread a large square of wrapping paper on the table, pattern side down (white side up).
2. With a permanent marker, fill up the white side of the wrapping paper with small drawn designs and doodles. A ruler or other straight edge will help make lines. Take as much time as needed, including rest periods for a tired drawing hand or arm. Some design ideas include:

   - checks or checkers
   - dots
   - flowers
   - herringbones
   - lines
   - little letters
   - little numbers
   - plaid
   - squiggles
   - stars
   - swirls
   - triangles

3. With scissors, cut the patterned wrapping paper into wide strips from one side to the other, approximately 6 to 8 strips each 2" to 4" (6cm to 12cm) wide. Wrap all the strips around a stick, dowel, or broom handle and secure with a rubber band to make them curl. Set aside briefly.
4. Tape a paper towel tube in a standing position to the square of cardboard. Use as much tape as needed to make it stand strong. This will be the center of the structure that supports the curls of paper.
5. Remove the curls from the stick. Begin with one curl of paper, and loop and curl it around the tube so that both sides of the paper show, both the patterned gift wrap and the drawn designs. Tape it to hold. Add a second curl, looping and curling once again and taping in place. Use all the curls of paper. Cover the tube completely, or leave part of the tube exposed.
6. When complete, stand back and admire the looping sculpture. Adjust the loops, if needed.

For Budding Artists

- Scrunch newspaper into balls.
- Tape scraps of paper to a cardboard square.
- Curl paper strips around a dowel.

Crinkle Scruncher

Scrunch and crinkle paper into forms that can be hanging sculptures or standing figures.

Materials

thin paper, such as newsprint or colorful origami paper

    (Crinkled paper can be purchased from craft and school supply stores. Shredded paper is often available from the recycle bin at local printing shops or from offices.)

scissors

colorful thread, yarn, or string

glue (optional)

cardboard square (optional)

Process

1. Crinkle and scrunch paper (or use pre-crinkled paper) into forms and shapes. Squeezing and scrunching the paper will soften it and make it more pliable.
2. Make several shapes or forms that hold together.
3. Wind, wrap, and bind the crinkled shapes with colorful thread, yarn, or string. Shapes can be tied to hold a desired form, or tied and joined to other shapes. Shapes may also be joined to form a figure, animal, or creature.
4. Hang the finished form by a thread to display, or glue to a heavy cardboard base.

On Fire for Wire!

Get to know wire and how it bends and forms in this easy-to-do sculpting experience.

Materials

florist wire or other easily bendable craft wire (hobby or craft store)

Styrofoam block (saved from packing material)

yarn, variety of colors

scissors

Process

1. Bend a wire into a simple shape. Try making curls, loops, square angles, and zigzag bends. Stick one end of the bent wire into the Styrofoam. Then stick in the other end. Push ends deep into the Styrofoam.

2. Add more wires in the same way, creating a wire sculpture of abstract shapes. No glue or tape is needed.

3. For added design and color, tie yarn from one wire to another, or weave colorful strands of yarn in and out of wire forms.

Wire Ideas

- Push wires into a Styrofoam coffee cup to make a small sculpture.
- "Sew" wire in and through a Styrofoam grocery tray.

For Budding Artists

- Bend pipe cleaners or fuzzy chenille wires into shapes.

Wire 'n Wood

Create a curly, twisty, whimsical wire sculpture secured in a block of wood.

Materials

small nail, slightly smaller in diameter than the wire
multicolored wires (recycle from telephone installation or repair)
hammer
wood block
glue
safety goggles

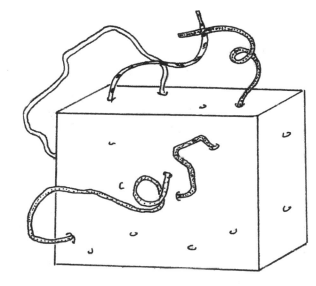

Process

1. With adult help and supervision, hammer a nail about ¼" (1 cm) into the wood block several times to make a pattern of holes in the top. (Always wear safety goggles when using a hammer.)

2. Add a dot of glue to the end of the wire before inserting it in the hole. Insert one end of a wire into a hole.

3. Bend, twist, and shape the wire, leave it poking out, or insert the other end of it into another hole. Add more wires as desired, letting them poke out of the holes or twisting them around and attaching them to the other wires. The sculpture can be abstract or can form something recognizable, such as an animal or familiar object.

Wire Sculpture Ideas

- Paint the wooden block before the sculpting steps.
- Insert wire into sides and edges of the wood block as well as the top.

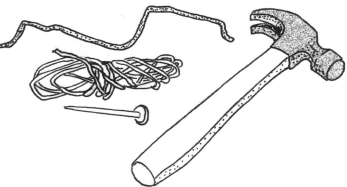

I'm Wired!

Create a wire figure with a wrapping technique, building thickness and features where wire is wrapped heaviest.

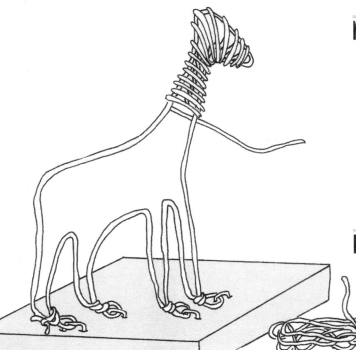

Materials

heavy gauge wire, about 3′ (1m)

pliers

hammer

block of wood

stapler

thin, colored wire

scissors

wire cutter (adult only)

Process

1. Choose to sculpt a human, animal, or abstract form. Begin with the heavy gauge wire. Bend the wire in one piece into the basic form or skeleton. Does it have two legs or four? A long neck or short? Bend until it holds the skeleton or basic shape.

2. Bend the wire feet of the form with pliers or by hand (see illustration) into small loops or "Ls." If a hammer is needed to help bend the wire, hammer the wire directly on the wood. Staple the feet of the wire to the block of wood. Use as many staples as needed. (Adult help and/or supervision may be needed with this step.)

3. To fill out the form's shape, begin wrapping colored wire around and around the base form. Add more and more wire, building the thickness of the shape where needed. Bend and twist wires to add details like hair or ears.

Hint: The base wire will be virtually hidden by colored wire.

For Budding Artists

- Wind a pipe cleaner around a crayon or pencil to make a curl, and slide it off.
- Join two paper shapes together with a stapler.
- Join two paper shapes together with a metal brad.

People Posing

Create a human figure in costume, with arms and legs that pose in different positions.

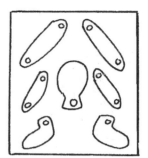

Materials

tagboard or other stiff
   paper
hole punch
metal brads

crayons and markers
glue
bamboo skewer
tape
small block of Styrofoam

decorations, such as:
   beads
   fabric scraps
   feathers
   wiggle eyes
   sequins
   yarn

Process

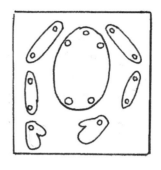

1. Draw separated body parts for a human figure on tagboard (see illustration). Include two upper arms, two lower arms, two thighs, two lower legs, one torso, one head, two hands, and two feet. Draw the parts at least 1" (3cm) wide.

2. Cut out the body part shapes. Overlap them at the "joints" where the pieces will join together (knees, elbows, and other parts of the body). Punch holes through both overlapped pieces at one time. Insert a brad into each hole to join the pieces together. Bend out the two prongs of the brad to hold the joints together.

3. With fabric, yarn, sequins, feathers, and beads, design costumes or clothing for the figure. Add yarn and wiggle eyes for hairdos and face.

4. Color in the figure with crayons and markers.

5. Pose the figure in different positions. When satisfied with a pose, tape the figure to a bamboo skewer. Push the skewer into the Styrofoam block as a display technique. If the sculpture falls over, the block may need a bit more weight. Try a larger block, or attach something heavy to the bottom of the block.

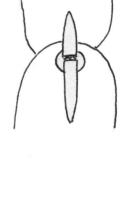

Solo Abstract

Create an abstract sculpture with scrunched newspaper shapes wrapped with masking tape, and then covered with papier-mâché. Display atop a solo perch in a Styrofoam block.

Materials

newsprint or newspaper	narrow dowel or thin	nail, screwdriver, or other
masking tape	wooden skewer	poking tool
papier-mâché paste	Styrofoam block or cube	tempera paints or acrylic
(see p. 175)	white glue (hot glue	paints
	optional, adult only)	paintbrush

Process

1. Make a free-form shape by squeezing and forming balls, wads, and cones of newspaper or newsprint. Tape them together with masking tape to form the abstract shape.
2. Tear other newspaper or newsprint into strips.
3. Dip the newspaper strips into the papier-mâché paste and apply to the abstract form. Smooth with fingers to remove wrinkles and bubbles. Then apply a second layer. Again, smooth the papier-mâché. Let dry one full day. Add a third coat of papier-mâché. At this time, add bits of newspaper to build up any details with papier-mâché. Dry overnight or two days. The sculpture should be very dry.
4. If a display format is desired, push one end of a narrow dowel or pencil into a Styrofoam block to form a display mode or leg to stand on to support the shape. Add glue around the base of the dowel. Make a hole in the abstract shape with a nail or other poking tool. Add extra glue to the hole and insert the dowel.
5. Paint the shape in abstract designs. Dry again and display.

Hint: The form may be displayed without the stick and block by simply arranging it on a table or shelf.

For Budding Artists

- Scrunch newspaper into balls. Tape them to hold their shapes.
- Cover newspaper balls with papier-mâché.

Long Leggity Thing

Create a papier-mâché balloon sculpture with silly bamboo stick legs.

Materials

medium (6"-7") latex balloon for each creature
small wooden block
bamboo skewers or thin wooden skewer
white glue or tacky glue
decorations (see step 6)

materials for adding appendages, such as:
  aluminum foil
  cardboard or tagboard scraps
  masking tape
  newspaper
  paper towel tube

strips of newspaper
papier-mâché paste (see directions on page 175)
electric drill (or hammer and small nail), adult supervision required

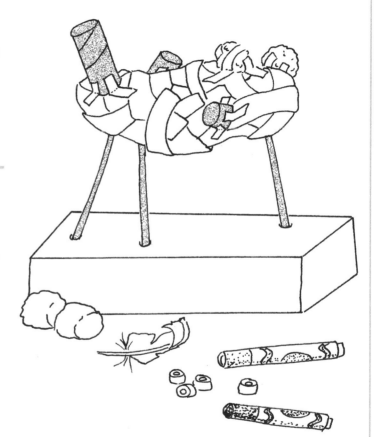

Process

1. With adult help, blow up a balloon to the size preferred. Add choices of wild attachments to the "long leggity" made from paper towel tubes. Cut a tube into sections and tape to the balloon with masking tape, making legs, arms, or any silly appendages. (Bamboo skewers will be added later.)

2. To make "bumpy" features, squeeze aluminum foil or balls of newspaper into forms or shapes, and attach to the balloon (or to the cardboard tube) with masking tape. Cardboard and/or tagboard pieces can be taped on now.

3. Cover the balloon with at least two layers of newspaper strips dipped in the papier-mâché paste. Dip the newspaper in the paste, and then squeeze off extra with fingers. Press the strips on the balloon, overlapping pieces.

4. More features and appendages can be attached at this stage. To do this, cut cardboard or tagboard pieces; cover them with papier-mâché newspaper strips, pasting and securing them directly to the sculpture. Allow the sculpture to dry until hard—two or three days is usual.

5. Meanwhile, with adult help and/or supervision, make the base. Drill or hammer two or more small holes in the wooden block, one for each long bamboo skewer selected for the sculpture. Insert blunt ends of the bamboo skewers into each hole with a drop of glue. Work the pointy ends of the skewers into the underside of the balloon, poking through the papier-mâché. Push skewers deep enough into the balloon shape so the sculpture can stand on its own long bamboo legs (two or more). Stabalize with some extra glue or tape.

6. Add final decorations, such as glitter paints, pearlescent acrylics, puffy paints, and metallic markers. Sequins, feathers, buttons, beads, cotton balls, and other materials may be added with drops of glue. Add some decorations around the base of each skewer where it joins the wooden block.

Alternative Display Idea
Hang the sculpture (base omitted) from fishing line tied to a pushpin in the ceiling, window casing or doorframe.

Little Thingamajigs

With this wonderfully workable colored salt dough, sculpt, invent, and create a group of little creatures, critters, bugs, animals, people, or any imaginable objects.

Materials

colored salt dough (see recipe on page 175)	selection of tools for sculpting, such as:
wooden board, foil, or wax paper	dull knife
baking sheet	fork
oven	garlic press
small cup of water	paper clip
hobby coating or varnish and brush (optional)	small rolling pin
	toothpick

Process

1. Make the colored salt dough. Mix and knead the dough until soft, smooth, and pliable. Working on a wooden board, foil, or wax paper, explore and play with the dough, finding out how it models and behaves. Try rolling, pinching, fringing, squeezing, cutting and forming. Then roll all the experiments into balls, and start creating one or many Little Thingamajigs.

2. Work with pinches and small portions of dough at a time. Different parts, such as legs and arms, can be joined to other dough pieces by pressing them together with a toothpick or paper clip. With a wet finger, smooth the joints where colors and pieces join. Designs and features can be carved or etched with a toothpick or other tool. A garlic press makes hair to press onto the object with a toothpick.

3. Place each Thingamajig on the baking sheet to air dry or bake. When hard and dry, brush with hobby coating or varnish to add shine and help preserve the Little Thingamajig.

For Budding Artists

- Explore with any playdough or play clay, using tools to make impressions and designs.

Fantasy Island Map

Create a fantasy island on a square of plywood with a modified salt dough recipe that is perfect for building a map with mountains, coves, roads, rivers, and lakes.

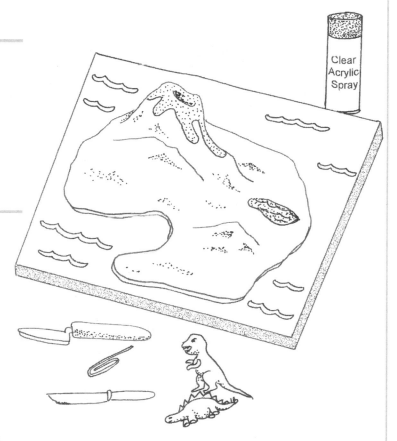

Materials

map salt dough (see recipe on page 176)

square of plywood (or heavy cardboard), suggested size 1 yd (1m) square

putty knife or spatula for spreading dough

mix additional colored dough (see page 175)

sculpting tools (see page 150)

clear acrylic spray paint (optional, adult step)

Process

1. Mix the map salt dough in a quantity large enough to cover the board. Also mix a batch of Colored Salt Dough for extra features.

2. Think of a fantasy world or island to build on the board. Will it have mountains, a volcano, lakes or coves, rivers, forests, beaches, or rocks? Remember, if making an island, surround the land with water.

3. Spread the map dough over the entire board with a spatula or putty knife. Use any color preferred. Green works well for grass and forested areas, blue for water, and white for crashing waves, snow, or beaches. When the basic island is spread on the board, add additional colored salt dough to build taller features like mountains and hills. Sculpt and cut in deep features like canyons and riverbeds. Add dough trees, rocks, pathways, and so on. Etch details in the dough with a toothpick or paper clip.

4. Add a few little plastic toys, such as cars, animals, or people, if desired. Press them right into the dough, or stand them on the surface.

5. The fantasy island will dry in 1–3 days to a very hard consistency, and will keep indefinitely. A light coating of clear acrylic paint may be sprayed on it by an adult, but is not required.

Associated Clay

Add interest and dimension to a drawing with clay objects that complement the theme.

Materials

thick paper

paint or pens

glue

commercial dough or clay that hardens when baked, such as Fimo™, Sculpey™, or homemade cornstarch dough (see recipe on page 176)

oven

Process

1. Draw or paint a simple subject or picture in the center of the thick paper. For example, paint an apple tree.

2. If using commercial Fimo™ or Sculpey™, create matching objects to complement the picture from the choices of colors available. Bake according to package directions to a hard consistency. If using cornstarch dough, first bake or air dry the objects, and then use tempera or acrylic paints to color them.

3. Glue three-dimensional clay or dough objects directly to the painting. For the apple tree example, glue Fimo™ sculpted apples to the tree, border, or to further highlight in any way.

Theme Suggestions

● Self-portrait painting: add clay hair, glasses, earrings, buttons

● Pet drawing: add clay toy, collar, bone, pet tag

● Undersea drawing: add clay shells, pirate treasure, seaweed

● Holiday painting: add clay symbols like hearts, reindeer, shamrocks, bunnies

For Budding Artists

● Explore playing and modeling with cornstarch dough and other playdoughs. Air dry or bake in a warm oven.

Fancy Clay Plaque

Work with real clay to create an unusual air-dried plaque incorporating beads, stones, and wire.

Materials

moist clay (also called earth clay or real clay, from a craft store)

wooden board, or other covered work surface

clay tools (roller, plastic knife, poking tool)

beads or stones with holes for stringing (homemade or purchased)

craft wire, thin or lightweight

work scissors or wire cutter (adult help needed)

hobby coating and brush, or clear acrylic spray paint (adult step)

Hint: If colored beads are preferred, make them ahead of time (see step 3 below), dry, and paint with acrylic paints for permanent color, or tempera paint for matte color.

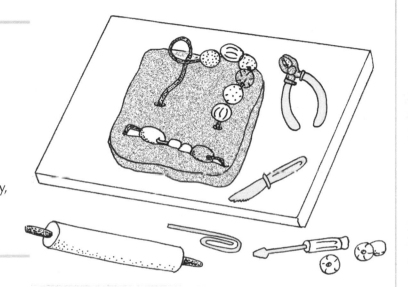

Process

1. Prepare a work area for clay. Work on a board for easier cleanup.

2. Roll a ball or slab of clay into a flat shape that will be the plaque and base for the project. A good size is 5" x 5" (10cm x 10cm). Set aside.

3. Use purchased beads, or form beads and stones from clay. Push a poking tool (toothpick, paper clip) through each bead for stringing. Etch in further details and designs with the poking tool.

4. String the beads on wire. With adult help, use work scissors or a wire cutter if needed. String one wire, or create multiple wires with beads. Poke the ends of the wires through the clay plaque to the back. Curl the ends of the wire to form a knot. Let the plaque artwork air-dry undisturbed for several days.

5. When dry, an adult can coat the plaque with hobby coating or spray with clear acrylic paint to seal and shine. (Work in ventilated area.) Dry until no longer sticky to the touch.

More Information About Moist Clay

Read the storage directions on the clay's bag or box label. Clay can be wrapped in plastic and saved over a long period of time. If it dries out, add water to refresh. Check directions and suggestions on the label.

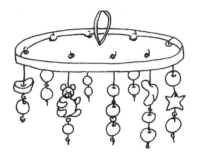

Windy Bead Mobile

Beads made from a superior salt dough recipe are strung on fishing line from a plastic coffee can lid to create a charming mobile.

Materials

salt dough (see recipe on page 176)	yarn or fishing line
toothpick or drinking straw to make holes	scissors
	coffee can plastic snap-on lid
oven and cookie sheet (optional)	hole punch
foil or wax paper	paints and brushes, or markers

Process

1. Form beads and objects with the salt dough. With a toothpick or drinking straw, poke a hole all the way through the bead, or make a hole top and bottom in other objects. (See illustrations.)

2. Choose to air dry or bake.
   - **To air dry:** Place on foil or wax paper. Turn over each day for two or three days until dry.
   - **To bake:** Place on a foil-lined cookie sheet and bake at 325°F (160°C) for 1 hour or until dry, hard, and hollow sounding when tapped with a knife. Cool.

3. Paint or color with markers.

4. While the salt dough beads or objects dry and/or cool, prepare the hanging device. Punch holes around the entire edge or rim of a plastic coffee can snap-on lid. (Save the punch-outs for another project.) Double-knot yarn or fishing line through each hole. Decide which part of the lid will be the top, and add some extra line to make a hanging loop.

5. String beads and objects on the pre-knotted line, double-knotting each one for good hold. Hang indoors in an area where air currents or wind will move the mobile gently. Or hang outdoors in a dry area, such as a porch or entryway.

For Budding Artists

- Make a small object, figure, or ornament with Salt Dough. Air dry or bake. Paint with tempera paints.

Jellie Dangles

Plain gelatin is transformed into unusual, solid gummy shapes that hang from threads.

Materials

2 envelopes unflavored gelatin, plain
glass, liquid measuring cup
6 T. boiling water (adult only)
choice of coloring agents, such as:
    acrylic paints
    food coloring or paste coloring
    Liquid Watercolors™
    tempera paints

choices of molds, such as:
    bottle caps
    commercial candy molds
    plastic lids
    Styrofoam egg carton cups
spoon
paper clip or toothpick
yarn or strong thread
stick
scissors

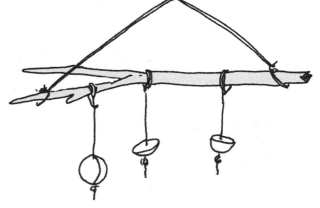

Process

1. Empty both envelopes of unflavored gelatin into a glass measuring cup. An adult can measure 6 tablespoons boiling water into the gelatin. Add a few drops of the chosen coloring agent, such as food coloring or paint. Stir quickly to dissolve.

2. Spoon the gelatin mixture into plastic lids, bottle caps, or other small molds. Dry overnight or as long as several days. When the shapes (the jellies) start to set, poke a hole in each with a toothpick or paper clip for stringing later.

3. When the jellies are completely dry, pop them out of the lids or caps. String yarn or thread through each jellie. Tie all the dangling jellies to a stick, moving and adjusting how the jellies dangle and balance.

4. Tie one more piece of yarn from one end of the stick to the other (see illustration) forming a hanging device. Display the dangling jellies and enjoy them.

Fancy Gift Folder

Using a basic template or one's own design, create a gift folder from decorated stiff paper suitable for hiding flat gifts such as handmade paper, scarves, or bandanas, or other homemade surprises.

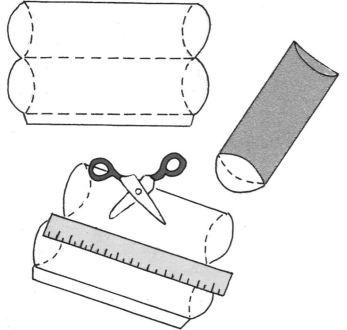

Materials

gift folder pattern (see illustration)
pencil, ruler, or straight edge
scissors
stiff paper or tagboard
glue

tape
decorating materials, such as:
    spray bottle filled with thin paint
    cut-out shape(s)

Process

1. Choose to trace the gift folder pattern on the back of the stiff paper, or create an original folded-design holder.
2. Use a ruler or straight edge to draw the folding line.
3. Then cut out the pattern and score the lines with the points of a scissors held against a ruler.
4. Turn the folder to the right side. Fold the stiff paper on the scored lines.
5. Stick the glue flap to the side of the folder.
6. Decorate the folder as follows, or choose another idea: Place the cut-out shape on the folder. Spray it lightly with the paint. Dry for a few seconds. Then lift the cutout. A stencil print will remain. Choose to make more stencil prints, or use just one. Dry completely.
7. Place a gift in the folder.
8. Close the ends of the folder by folding in the curved top and bottom. They will pop into place without glue or tape.

Decorating Ideas

- Create a simple collage on the folder using magazine clippings.
- Tie the folder with fancy ribbon.
- Add a gift tag to the folder.
- Wrap the folder with colored masking tape in overlapping, woven designs.
- Before forming the folder with the glue flap, choose a permanent marker and draw small designs and images over the entire folder. Then glue, fill, and close.

For Budding Artists

- Fold paper into self-styled envelopes and staple or glue.
- Glue collage materials into a shoebox lid in a design or pattern.

One & Only Art Box

Construct an artistic display box to express the artist's unique individuality.

Materials

wooden, cardboard, or plastic sectioned box

choices of decorative art materials, such as those listed on page 13

other materials, such as:

beads	pictures	puffy paint pens
buttons	small mementos	sequins
confetti	writings	glue, tape, string
feathers	metallic pens	dried flowers
glitter	paint	paintings
hole punch dots	postcards	photos

Process

1. Turn the box on its side or stand on one end so that it forms a "display case." Sections or dividers will form shelves and boxes. Decorate the background and interior of the box with paint, postcards, or colored paper.

2. Arrange the chosen items in the box to display in sections or shelves. Items can be propped up, hung from string, stacked, or glued to stand alone. Any kind of display is effective, such as a scene, an abstract arrangement or design, a sorted and grouped collection, or an expression of the artist's choice.

Themes and Decorating Ideas

- Group a variety of boxes, with or without sections, and assemble pictures, objects, items, writing, paintings, or collectibles of choice in the box or the box's sections.
- Fill each section of a box with a progressive display of photographs that tell a story or catalog the years of someone's life.
- Design a "theme" box, such as items and pictures displayed by color, function, holiday, hobbies, travel, family, pets, seasons, or shapes.
- A group of artists can stack boxes together to create a group display.

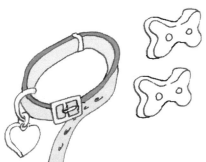

Display Idea

- Little balls of clay or dough work well for sticking objects to shelves.

Embossing System

A cardboard relief with two levels becomes the base for a simple embossed paper design.

Materials

glue	heavy paper
cardboard scraps	sponges
cardboard or matte board square for background	water
	craft sticks
scissors	map pins
varnish and varnish brush (adult only)	

Process

1. Glue large cardboard shapes and pieces to the background cardboard, creating the first level.
2. Next, glue a second layer of smaller cardboard shapes over the first layer. Be sure shapes from both levels are visible.
3. An adult can paint the finished cardboard collage with varnish to keep it from soaking up moisture or getting wet. Varnish must dry thoroughly.
4. Wet a sheet of heavy paper on both sides with a sponge. Place the wet paper over the cardboard design and press down from the center out. Use craft sticks to gently rub it down and press into the details of the collage behind it. Shapes from the cardboard will press into the paper leaving a raised design.
5. Gently lift the paper from the collage and set aside to dry. When dry, display with map pins on a board or on the wall.

Hint: Both the collage and the embossed paper are works of art.

Color Ideas

- With watercolor paint, highlight parts of the wet—or dry—embossed design. Paint will soak and blur into the paper.
- Trace or highlight shapes in the embossed design with colored or metallic markers.
- Glue dots of sequins or paper punch holes to the embossed design.

For Budding Artists

- Glue cardboard scraps on a cardboard background.
- Glue paper scraps and collage materials on a matte board background.

Stratum Relief

Create a matte-board relief with three or more layers, building a design with increased levels of detail.

Materials

matte board or cardboard

scissors

glue

poster board scraps

tempera paints and paintbrush or colored markers

layer 1
layer 2
layer 3

Process

1. Think of a design or picture to create with pieces of poster board scraps that build in layers. Think about how the broadest details will be layered first, and the smaller and finer details will be layered second and third. A few general ideas are:
   - face of person or character
   - face of animal or pet
   - flowers
   - fish with scales
   - sky with stars, moons, planets
   - abstract design

   (As an example, a vase of flowers is described in this activity.)

2. Start on a large piece of cardboard or matte board.

3. Layer 1: Cut out and glue the largest and least detailed part of the vase, some stems, and some leaves to the background.

4. Layer 2: Cut out and glue on shapes for more leaves and petals of the flowers.

5. Layer 3: Add details to the petals and leaves with additional poster board scrap pieces.

6. When all the layers are done, let the glue dry briefly. The layered art can be painted with tempera paints, colored with markers, or left as it is.

Hint: Painting the entire relief white or gray is a subtle artistic expression.

Wrap It "Op"

Wrap a familiar object in fancy papers, altering the appearance but retaining the shape. Very "op art!"

Materials

item to wrap, such as a teapot, shoe, hammer, or any other object with an obvious and interesting shape

choices of ties, such as:
- ribbon
- string
- yarn
- colorful tape
- surveyor or construction ribbon (on a roll)

choices of wrappings and paper, such as:
- aluminum foil
- art tissue
- classified pages
- fabric
- gift wrap
- painted paper

scissors

glue, tape, stapler

Process

1. Select an item to wrap, an object whose shape will be obvious and interesting. Some examples are a teapot, a hammer, a lamp, a saucepan, or a shoe.
2. Spread out materials for wrapping and tying. Suggestions for wrapping materials include:
   - traditional gift wrap, or something more unusual like newspaper or aluminum foil.
   - individual wrapping paper made with finger painting, printing, doodling, or plain paper decorated with colors and designs.
3. Wrap the item. Tie and form it to enhance its shape.
4. Display on a shelf or table. Others will enjoy guessing what it might be.
5. For extra fun, tie on a little tag that says something about the art: Title of op art, name of artist, directions for use of item, feelings or poem about item, or other ideas.

For Budding Artists

- Wrap a gift box or soup can in wrapping paper.
- Arrange plastic flowers in a coffee can.

Charming Shoe-In

Create an artful arrangement in a shoe or boot that expresses something about the artist or represents the artist's life.

Materials

collect assorted lengths of ¼" twigs and sticks found in the yard, park, or woods (other choices: narrow dowels or bamboo skewers)

old shoe or boot

gravel or sand

glue, tape, stapler

assorted mementos

materials for creating optional small works of art, such as:

    contact paper

    crayons

    dried flowers

    paint

    paper

    pens

Process

1. Collect about six to ten long twigs or narrow sticks outdoors. Bring them in and set aside.
2. Fill a favorite old shoe or boot with gravel or sand, which will support the art flags in steps 3 and 4.
3. Create "art flags." Glue, tape, or staple small artworks to each stick. Place the finished flags in the shoe like a flower arrangement. The flags will represent the person who made the sculpture. Further, attach other special objects or items to additional sticks.

Some Suggestions

- small baby sock that belonged to the artist
- leaf pressed between wax paper pieces
- melted crayon on paper
- self-portrait drawing
- small toy
- award
- photo

4. Place all the flags in the shoe and arrange similar to a flower arrangement. Use as a centerpiece or enjoy in any way.

Hint: At a later time, the objects can be returned to their original use; shoes will not be damaged or ruined.

Plaster & Fabric Pot

Making something out of nothing is a satisfying and creative endeavor. Transform a milk carton into a plaster-fabric container and useful decoration.

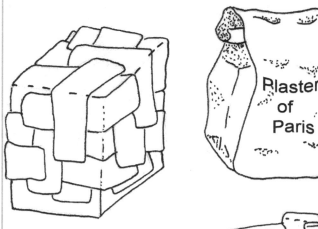

Materials

½ cup (118ml) plaster of Paris

¼ cup (60ml) cup water

small plastic bowl

spoon

strips of white or light colored fabric

milk carton, clean and dry

scissors

bucket

warm water

old towel or paper towels

tempera or acrylic paints, paintbrush

Process

1. Cut off the top of a milk carton (see illustration).

2. Mix ½ cup (118ml) plaster of Paris with ¼ cup (60ml) water in a small plastic bowl with a plastic spoon. Plaster should be the consistency of heavy cream. (Work quickly before plaster can harden.)

3. Dip strips (or squares) of white or light-colored fabric into the plaster. Press the wet fabric strips on a milk carton, working and overlapping the pieces slightly until the carton is covered. Then let it dry. (Plaster will harden and dry quickly.) Rinse hands in a bucket of warm water to remove plaster, and dry with paper towels or an old towel.

Hint: Do not wash plaster down the drain. It can seriously clog pipes. Place dry plaster scraps in the trash or crush and sprinkle in the garden to help aerate soil.

4. When completely dry, paint fancy designs and patterns with acrylic or tempera paints on the plaster covered carton. Let paint dry. Use the container for decoration or to hold special items. The container makes a great pencil jar!

For Budding Artists

- Cover a milk carton with strips of construction paper and glue.
- Glue collected and saved junk and collage materials on a wood scrap.

Gizmo Arrangement

Assemble and construct a sculpture with parts and pieces of just about anything joined with building hardware and tape.

Materials

choices of junk or broken gadgets and hardware, such as: auto/bike parts, coils, faucet, gears, hand eggbeater, hardware (miscellaneous), keyboard, kitchen utensils, manual typewriter, nuts and bolts, pepper grinder, plumbing fittings, springs tea strainer, toys, washers

choices of junk or broken and disabled electrical gizmos, such as: calculator, circuit board radio, toaster, typewriter
safety goggles
work gloves
strong cardboard box, at least 1' x 1' or larger (30cm x 30cm)
glue, or hot glue gun (adult help)

supplies, such as: wire, nails, screws, nuts and bolts, duct tape, masking tape
tools, such as: hammer, screwdriver, pliers, crescent wrench
decorating additions (optional), such as: wiggle craft eyes, ribbons, sewing trims, wood scraps

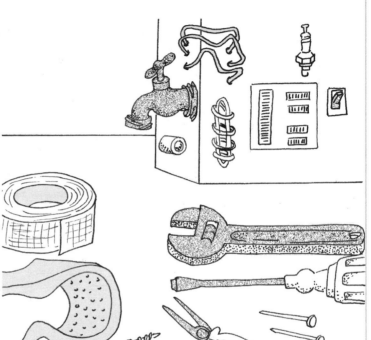

Process

Note: Adult help and supervision is required when using tools and hardware supplies.

1. Disassemble a broken gizmo or gadget (or several). Wear safety goggles and work gloves while working. The dismantled bits and pieces will be used to create a sculpture on the board.
2. To begin the sculpture, attach pieces to the box using any variety of methods, including: tape, glue, screws, wire, nails, or a hot glue gun. An excellent idea is to poke a hole in the box and insert part of the gizmo or gadget to hold.
3. Wood scraps or other building supplies may also be added to the sculpture.
4. If preferred, sewing trims and ribbons may be added. Wiggle craft eyes can give the sculpture personality.
5. When the box is full, the sculpture is complete.

Finishing Ideas

- Spray paint the entire sculpture with metallic paint. (Adult help and/or supervision is required.)
- Embellish the sculpture with glitter or metallic paint in selected areas.
- Cover and coat the entire sculpture with thick, clay-like white joint compound from a building supply store. Paint when dry, or leave white.

Capacitor Caution

A capacitor looks like a small can, or old-style battery with terminals on the top. Capacitors are found in TVs and home electronics. They store electricity and can be a small shock risk. To make the capacitor useless, an adult should touch its electrodes together with a plastic handled screwdriver. Though it is easy to do, it can be something new or intimidating for some. To skip or avoid, simply choose gizmos and gadgets that have no electrical parts and operate manually.

Knock, Knock, Build It

Design a building complete with windows and doors that open and close. Knock, knock, is anyone home?

Materials

large drawing paper	scissors
pencil, crayons or markers	tape
extra white paper	yellow tissue paper (optional)
ruler or straight edge	clear plastic wrap (optional)

Process

1. Think of a house or other building to design. Some considerations will be:
   - house, castle, skyscraper, school, or resort
   - one, two, or many floors
   - flat, pointed, or slanted roof
   - style of building: modern, old-fashioned, futuristic, or fantasy
   - colors, trims, and decorations
   - windows and doors
   - other: porch, chimney, skylights, flowers, car, curtains, and stairs

2. Using as much of the large paper as possible, lightly sketch the general idea of a large-shaped building, including where the floors, windows, doors, and roof will be. Then use a ruler to draw in more permanent lines. Color the building completely with crayon, markers, or both. Can be imaginary or realistic.

3. To cut windows, poke a tiny hole with the scissors or a paper clip on a corner of one window. Carefully poke the scissors into the hole, and cut the window out.

Hint: To make the windows and doors open and close, do the same, but leave part of the window attached to the wall so it opens and closes on the fold. Do the same for doors.

4. Is anyone home? Draw people, pets, or other characters on white squares of paper. Place them behind the window and tape in place so they can peek out the windows. For lighted or glass windows, tape yellow tissue or clear plastic wrap behind the windows.

5. Ideas to add:
   - draw features around the building or in the yard
   - draw small features on scrap paper, cut out, and tape to the building or yard
   - draw what could be inside each room on the reverse side of the building design

For Budding Artists

- Draw a house on paper with crayons. Cut holes for the windows with scissors.
- Build a village or town with wooden blocks.

Winter Village

Create a village in winter—or any time of year—from milk cartons covered in gesso, and decorated with paint, scraps, and glue.

Materials

milk cartons of various sizes (½ gallon, quart, pint)

gesso (white paint-like liquid great for covering print on boxes or cartons, available in art or hobby stores)

tempera paint and paintbrush

scissors (or X-acto knife, adult use only)

decorations, such as:
yellow tissue paper, construction paper, in assorted colors, cardboard, cotton balls, fiberfill, silver or white glitter, and small toys

large cardboard base (sheet of cardboard)

Process

1. Work in an area that can be dedicated to project use over a week or more.

2. Cut off the bottoms of the milk cartons. Paint the milk cartons with gesso in a smooth layer to cover all print and wax. Allow gesso to dry. Each milk carton can be designed into a house or building in a winter village. Larger cartons can be upright to make multiple-story houses, or turned on their sides to be stores, schools, or houses. Cut windows and doors into the milk cartons.

3. Suggestions for decorating the village buildings include:
   - **Painted exterior walls**: Paint the buildings with tempera paint and let dry.
   - **Siding**: Cut strips of colored construction paper and glue on, one next to the other like boards or siding.
   - **Shingles**: Overlap long strips of fringed paper to create shingles or cedar shakes.
   - **Lighted windows**: Glue squares of yellow tissue paper inside the cartons behind the open windows to look as if light is shining inside.
   - **Smoke**: Cotton balls can be pulled thin to make "smoke" for chimneys.
   - **Snow**: Pulled cotton or white fiberfill can simulate snow covering the yards and rooftops. Silver or white glitter makes the snow look frosty.

4. Place the finished houses on a large cardboard base to create a town or village scene. Decorate the sheet of cardboard with roads, streams, or other features.

5. Continue to create additional cutouts to make trees, fences, sidewalks, and so on. Toys can also be added for cars and people.

Lighting Idea
- To light the houses, string twinkle lights under the cardboard, and poke a light up through a hole into each building.

Hint: Any season can be the focus instead of winter. Coffee grounds look like dirt, colored sand looks like concrete or grass, shredded green paper looks like grass, and crinkled blue foil looks like water. A mirror looks like a pond. Blue hair gel on plastic wrap looks like water. Look around for more items that might work in the village. Half the fun is discovering new uses for common materials.

Box Sculpture

Collect large cardboard boxes and build a sculpture with a message to share.

Materials

large boxes
glue, twine, or tape
hot glue gun (adult help)
large nail or pencil
scissors

decorating choices, such as:
   colored markers
   glitter
   mementos or collected items
   paint
   pens
   photos or magazine cutouts
   wide permanent marker

Process

1. Create a box sculpture with large boxes stacked and joined together in an interesting shape or assembly. Think of ways to make the boxes balance in unexpected ways. Boxes may be joined together with glue, tape, twine, or a hot-glue gun (with adult assistance). Holes poked with a pencil or nail allow for twine to tie them together.

2. When the box sculpture is assembled, think of how to use the sides of the boxes to communicate a message or let others know about something important. For example, convey feeling like sadness, joy, or anger, or strong messages such as, "I Believe in Recycling!" "I Believe in Saving Animals!" "I Believe in Exercise!" "I Believe in Family!" Then represent the message with collage, paint, or slogans. Paint or further decorate the boxes in any chosen way.

   A few suggestions for Message Sharing
   - Create photo or picture collages on the sides of the boxes.
   - Paint pictures or designs on the boxes.
   - Affix decorations, mementos, or collected items.
   - Paint or write words or slogans.

3. Display the box sculpture where others can study, observe, and view it from all sides.

For Budding Artists

- Paint designs or pictures with tempera paints on a cardboard box.
- Make six drawings and glue each one to a different side of one cardboard box.

Six-Sided Art Cube

Fold the paper cube pattern to make a box with six sides of art that can be turned in different ways.

Materials

cube pattern (see illustration, and also template on page 177)

heavy paper

pencil

glue or tape

scissors

choices of design materials, such as colored paper, colored tape, magazine pictures

markers (black and colored), photos, thin collage items, and words or letters cut from magazines or newspaper

Process

1. Trace the cube pattern on heavy paper. On each space of the cube, think about drawing and gluing designs based on a theme. Abstract designs and colors can fill in some of the cube's sides, adding to the overall artistic nature of the cube. Some theme ideas include:

careers	food	holidays	outer space
family	happiness	music	pets
fashion	heroes	nature	sports

   For example, with a pet theme on one square, glue a picture of a dog; on the next square, draw a "dog of my dreams;" on another, glue pictures of toys or things dogs enjoy; continue filling in the six squares of the cube with designs or pictures that relate to dogs.

2. When all spaces are filled, cut out the cube pattern. Fold it on the lines of the pattern into a cube. Tape or glue the edges to hold its shape.

3. Display the cube, turning it to different sides each day or for special occasions.

Hint: Hang the cube from a string so all sides are visible at all times.

Portrait Idea

- Draw a person or character facing forward on one space of the cube. Draw the same person or character's right profile on the space to the right, the left profile on the space to the left, the top of the head on the top space, the bottom of the chin and neck on the bottom space. This could be done for any object, showing how it is viewed from all angles.

Stacking Idea

- Make three or more cubes. Stack them into a sculpture, like building with blocks. Tape or glue them together, or stack them loosely.

Cardboard Construct

Create a free-form sculpture with cardboard scraps—a beginning experience in engineering and architectural design.

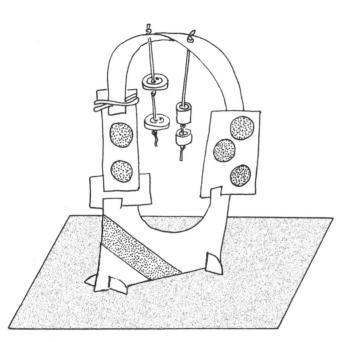

Materials

masking tape	decorating materials (optional), such as:
glue	beads
choice of strong scraps, such as:	buttons
cardboard	colored masking tape
matte board	colored rubber bands
poster board	labels
tagboard	markers
scissors	stickers
tempera paints	thread, string, yarn
paintbrushes	wire

Process

1. With tape or glue, join cardboard scraps together to build an abstract form, figure, architectural structure, or other sculpture idea (see illustration). Use scissors to shape scraps as needed. For extra hold, cut ½" to 1" (2cm to 3cm) slits into the edges of cardboard pieces, and slide the slits together. Reinforce with glue or tape.
2. When glue is dry and construction solid, paint with tempera paints or decorate with other decorating materials.

Construction and Decoration Ideas

- Build the construction on a square cardboard base, building the design upward.
- Use stickers or labels for decoration, windows and doors, patterns, or other colorful effects. Colored masking tape, rubber bands, and yarn add effective color.
- Add embellishments that dangle, hang, and swing using string, thread, or wire.
- Construct an architectural structure with cardboard scraps, such as a castle, house, factory, school, or building.

For Budding Artists

- Build houses with playing cards on the carpet.
- Make a playhouse out of an appliance box.

Walk-Through Sculpture

Stand big cardboard sheets and boxes in an arrangement that invites viewers to walk through a pathway of walls, reminiscent of a maze or an art gallery.

Materials

large cardboard scraps (cardboard, boxes, appliance boxes and large pieces of cardboard)
tempera paint and paintbrushes
tape, glue, stapler, duct tape, and masking tape

colored paper, scissors, glitter, and glitter pens
holiday twinkle lights
cloth strips

Process

1. Create a grouping of pieces of cardboard and boxes that can be walked between or through when complete, like a maze or gallery. Begin by cutting and folding cardboard. Large boxes, such as those from refrigerators or appliances, can be cut apart or left almost whole, lending themselves to passageways and doors.

2. Paint the cardboard inside and out as desired. Further decorate with tempera paints, colored paper cutouts, glitter, or glitter pens.

3. Arrange and stand all pieces of cardboard and boxes in a way that encourages paths between and through them, somewhat like a gallery with many walls and openings. Use duct tape, glue, stapler, and masking tape to join cardboard and make the structure strong and well reinforced.

4. Add holiday twinkle lights to embellish the artful display, especially when regular lights in the room are low. Simply drape the lights over the cardboard and shapes.

Safety Note: Keep electric wires out of traffic patterns.

5. Walk or crawl through the sculpture. Invite others to do the same.

Walk-Though Ideas

- **Scene Walk:** Bend large pieces of cardboard to make walls that will form hallways or dividers. Decorate the walls with scenes, such as the universe and outer space, an undersea world, or an imaginary word. Decorate or paint the scenery.
- **Story Walk:** Create a scenery walk that has a story. Tell the story while walking through the scenes. Take guided "tours" of the scenery walk.
- **Art Gallery:** Display artworks on all the sides of the walkway. Label the art with title, name, and price, just like a real gallery. Go on a gallery walk!

Wrapped Stick Sculpture

Wrap a stick with long strips and strands of an assortment of materials, and display as a wall sculpture.

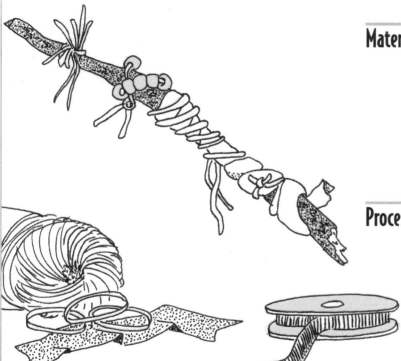

Materials

stick or dowel, about ½" to 1" thick (2cm to 3cm), any length (12" [30cm] works well)

scissors

pushpin or picture hanger

wrapping and weaving materials, such as:

beads
colored rubber bands
fuzzy chenille wires
metallic cord
pipe cleaners

raffia
ribbons
strips of fabric
surveyor's tape
yarn, unusual colors and fibers

Process

1. Find a stick outdoors and strip off the loose bark, or choose to use a plain wooden dowel.
2. Wrap the stick with choices of yarn, ribbon, raffia, and so on. Some art techniques to consider are:
   - cover the ends of the stick
   - form bows or pompoms
   - leave strands and tails hanging
   - string beads on strings, knot to secure
   - tie knots
   - tie one material to the next and wrap
   - twist different materials together
3. Fill the entire stick, or leave some natural wood showing.
4. When satisfied with the wrapping, hang the stick sculpture on a pushpin or picture hanger.

Sculpture Idea
- Make more than one stick sculpture and display as a unified sculpture group.

For Budding Artists

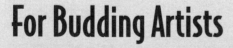

- Collect twigs and glue them to a piece of cardboard.
- Wrap a stick with yarn, round and round. Tie or tape.

Natural Grouping

Wrap a bundle of sticks with natural materials and display as an arrangement.

Materials

4–10 sticks, about ½" to 1" thick (2cm to 3cm), any length (remove or keep bark)

choice of natural wrapping and weaving materials, such as long grasses, raffia, strips cut from brown paper grocery bag, strips of natural fabric, twine or string, natural colors, yarn, natural colors and fibers, and other wrapping materials of choice

natural accessory materials, such as acorns, ceramic or homemade beads, natural feathers, pinecones, shells

container for display (terra cotta pot, basket, coffee can covered with natural fabric)

sand or rice to fill container (optional)

Process

1. Position a selection of sticks of similar size on the workspace. Hold them in place, and tie them all together with one strip of fabric or other material. Use knots and any wrapping or tying ideas.

2. Start wrapping and weaving natural materials through the sticks. Any technique has merit, so invent something new! Some ideas are:
   - wrap in and out between sticks
   - tie knots
   - twist different materials together
   - leave strands and tails hanging
   - cover the ends of the sticks
   - string beads, tie knots to secure
   - tie one material to the next and wrap
   - fray or fringe fabric strips

3. When the wrapping and weaving is complete, add accessories to the strands. String or tie on pinecones, shells, feathers, or beads. Tuck feathers or other materials into the threads.

4. Select a container to display the bundle. One suggestion is to cover a coffee can with natural fabric and tie with raffia to hold. Fill the can half-full of rice or sand to give it weight and support the bundle.

5. Insert the bundle into the can and display like a flower arrangement.

Favorite Framework

Frame a favorite mini-work of art with wooden craft sticks colored to match.

Materials

colored paper or a favorite mini-work of art (6" x 6" [15cm x 15cm] works well)

crayons

crayon stubs (peeled)

grater

newspaper

scissors

wooden craft sticks

old iron (adult assistance)

thick pad of newspaper

white glue in a squeeze bottle

choice of hanging device:
    pushpin, paperclip, tape

Process

1. Cut a square approximately 6" x 6" (15cm x 15cm). Draw a mini-work of art on the square with crayons. If preferred, select a formerly created small piece of art for this activity.

2. Look at the drawing and notice a strong color or several predominant colors in the art. Find these same colors of crayon stubs. Peel the stubs and grate (with adult help) onto newspaper. Keep the colors separate, or mix, whichever is preferred.

3. Make a thick pad of newspaper on the workspace with an electric iron within reach. Place 4–8 wooden craft sticks on the newspaper. Sprinkle grated crayon over the sticks lightly for minimal color or heavily for thick bright color.

4. Place another sheet of newspaper over the sticks. With adult help, press a warm iron set to "no steam" on the sticks. Press down solidly with only a little movement of the iron to melt the crayon into the sticks. Lift the newspaper. The sticks may adhere to the newspaper, but simply pull them free. Set aside briefly.

5. Outline the square of art all the way around with a medium-thin line of squeezed white glue, right next to the edge. Place a craft stick on each of the four sides in the glue, with tips touching. Some paper may extend beyond the frame. This can be trimmed later. Dry until the sticks hold firmly to the paper.

6. When dry, trim any excess paper from around the frame of sticks.

7. To hang the framed work, push a pushpin into the wall. Tape a paperclip to the back center top of the frame. Hang the art by the placing the paperclip on the pin.

For Budding Artists

- Glue collage items to the rim of a drawing or painting to suggest a frame.
- Paint on newsprint with one color of thin tempera paint.

Tatami Shoji Screen

Shoji screens are functional room dividers that provide privacy and diffuse light. Create a folding group of three mini-model Tatami shoji screens made from painted newsprint glued to wooden craft stick frames.

Materials

examples of Shoji screens (use books, Internet, art catalogs)

sheets of newsprint (rice paper for authentic screens)

black tempera paint or watercolor paint

small paintbrush

jar of water

tongue depressors, wooden craft sticks, or Popsicle sticks

white glue

scissors

pieces of leather or cording for hinges

hot glue gun (adult step)

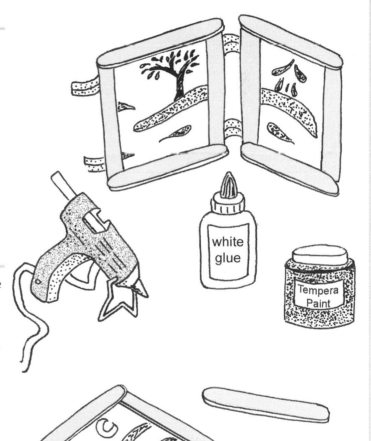

Process

1. **Getting ready**: Look at Shoji screen examples in books, on the Internet, or in Japanese art catalogs. Note the brush strokes and subject matter of traditional screens. Practice painting on newsprint, exploring the simple brush strokes of Japanese screen art.
2. On the newsprint, paint a series of three screen scenes that go together as one picture. Use simple brush strokes and black tempera or watercolor paint.
3. Trim all three paintings to the same size, about 6" x 8" (15cm x 20cm). Glue wooden craft sticks to the edges of each rectangle to construct frames for the paintings. Sticks may need to be overlapped a little when gluing if they are not long enough to cover the entire edge of the rectangle. Leave the paintings and their frames to dry overnight.
4. Turn all three paintings and their frames over to ready them for connecting hinges. Snip four scraps of leather or four short lengths of cording to about 1" (3cm). With adult help, use a hot glue gun to affix two hinges from the middle frame over to frames on the right and left. Stand the screens in a zigzag fashion to display.

Rice Paper Alternative
● Practice painting on newsprint, but make final screen paintings on rice paper for an authentic look.

Recipes

Flour Paste

Materials

1 cup water (237 ml)

1 cup flour (237 ml)

4 teaspoons (15 ml) alum (in the supermarket spice aisle)

measuring cups and spoons

electric mixer or blender

squeeze bottle (picnic ketchup type or shampoo)

Process

1. With adult help, make flour paste.
2. Start with 1 cup water.
3. Add 1 cup flour and 4 teaspoons alum. Mix with an electric mixer or blender until smooth. Pour the paste into a squeeze bottle.

Salt Solution

Materials

Epsom salts

measuring cup

water

saucepan and stovetop or heat plate

jar with lid

Process

1. With adult help, make the Salt Solution.
2. Fill a measuring cup with water. Pour in saucepan.
3. Add an equal amount of Epsom salts to the water. (For example: 1 cup (237 ml) water and 1 cup (237 ml) Epsom salts, or 3 cups (700 ml) water and 3 cups (700 ml) Epsom salts.)
4. Heat on the stove, stirring the salt as it dissolves. Some salt may not dissolve, which is to be expected. Let cool.
5. Pour the solution into a jar. Keep the lid handy to store unused solution.

Papier-Mâché Paste

Materials

flour

water

measuring cups

bowl

mixing spoon

saucepan

stovetop

sugar

measuring spoons

Process

1. With adult help, combine ½ cup (118 ml) flour with 2 cups (474 ml) cold water in a bowl.
2. Boil 2 cups (474 ml) of water in a saucepan, and then add the four-cold water mixture to the boiling water. Boil again.
3. Remove from heat. Stir in 3 tablespoons (45 ml) sugar. Let cool (it thickens as it cools).
4. Use with newspaper strips and squares.

Colored Salt Dough Recipe

Materials

flour

salt

measuring cups

bowl

mixing spoon

warm water

cutting board

food coloring, Liquid Watercolors™, tempera or acrylic paint

Process

1. Measure 4 cups (748 ml) flour and 1 cup (237 ml) salt in a mixing bowl.
2. Add 1½ cups (355 ml) warm water, mixing by hand until it forms a ball.
3. Knead on a cutting board until smooth and pliable.
4. Divide into individual balls, one for each color desired. Push a thumb into each ball of dough. Choose a coloring agent (food coloring, food coloring paste, Liquid Watercolors acrylic paint, tempera paint). Drop or squeeze a little color into the indentation. Knead the ball to mix evenly into the dough. If needed, add more color to increase intensity and brightness.

Map Salt Dough Recipe

Materials

salt
flour
water
measuring cup
large bowl
wooden spoon
small bowls

Process

1. In a large mixing bowl, mix 2 parts salt, 1 part flour, and 1 part water with a wooden spoon.
2. Mix to the consistency of spreadable cake icing. If desired, separate portions into small bowls to color individually with food coloring or paint.

Cornstarch Dough Recipe

(This recipe produces dough that is perfectly white and slightly grainy. Air-dry or bake in an oven. Recipe may be doubled or tripled.)

Materials

salt
water
measuring cups
saucepan
stove or hot plate
bowl
cornstarch
water
cutting board

Process

1. Mix ½ cup (118 ml) salt with ½ cup (118 ml) hot water in a saucepan.
2. With adult help and supervision, bring it to a boil.
3. Pour ½ cup (118 ml) cornstarch in a bowl, and then stir in ¼ (59 ml) cup cold water.
4. Add the cornstarch mixture to the hot salt water.
5. With adult help, cook over low heat, stirring until the mixture becomes the consistency of pie dough.
6. Turn out on a board. Cool. Then knead until smooth.
7. Air dry sculpted objects one to two days, or speed-bake for 1 hour at 200°F (90°C).

Salt Dough Recipe

Materials

salt
flour
water
measuring cups
bowl
mixing spoon

Process

1. Mix 1 part salt, 4 parts flour, and 1-2 parts water.
2. Knead well.
3. Bake 1 hour at 325°F (160°C), or air dry several days, turning each day until dry.

Six-Sided Art Cube

May be enlarged to any size.

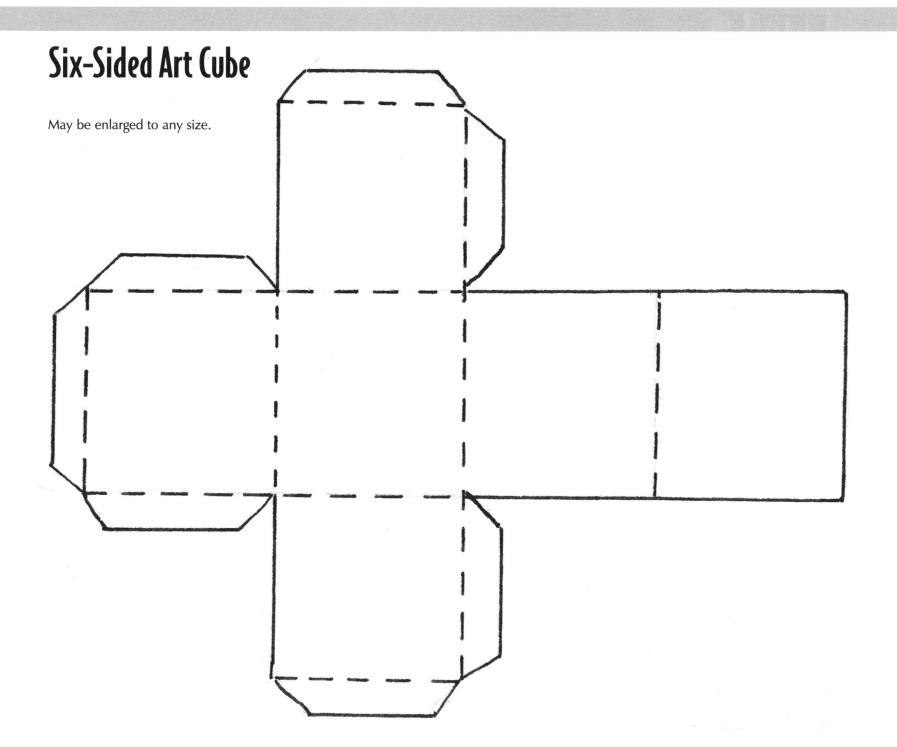

Indexes

Projects List

Project Index (by main art material & technique)

A